Make
My Life
A Prayer

Keith Green

Introduction by Melody Green

HARVEST HOUSE PUBLISHERS
Eugene, Oregon 97402

Cover by Koechel Peterson & Associates, Minneapolis, Minnesota

MAKE MY LIFE A PRAYER
Copyright © 2001 by Melody Green
Published by Harvest House Publishers
Eugene, Oregon 97402

Library of Congress Cataloging-in-Publication Data

Green, Keith, 1953-1982
    Make my life a prayer / Keith Green.
        p. cm.
    ISBN 0-7369-0360-7 (Hardcover edition)
    ISBN 0-7369-0949-4 (International edition)
    1. Christian life. I. Title.

BV4501.3 .G74 2001
248.4—dc21   2001024510

Printed in the United States of America.

01 02 03 04 05 06 07 08 09 10 / DC-MS / 10 9 8 7 6 5 4 3 2 1

Contents

To Rebekah Joy Green

*Your father cried out to God to
make his life a prayer—it brings me great joy
that you've chosen to do the same.*

—Mom

Make My Life a Prayer to You

Make my life a prayer to You
I wanna do what You want me to
No empty words and no white lies
No token prayers, no compromise

I wanna shine the light You gave
Through Your Son You sent to save us
From ourselves and our despair
It comforts me to know You're really there

Well I wanna thank You now
For being patient with me
Oh it's so hard to see
When my eyes are on me
I guess I'll have to trust
And just believe what You say
Oh You're coming again
Coming to take me away

I wanna die and let You give
Your life to me so I might live
And share the hope You gave me
The love that set me free

I wanna tell the world out there
You're not some fable or fairy tale
That I've made up inside my head
You're God the Son and You've risen from the dead

I wanna die and let You give
Your life to me so I might live
And share the hope You gave me
I wanna share the love that set me free

—Words and Music by Melody Green

The Testimony of a Life

Keith Green was an extraordinary man. His message and method were, and still are, unlike that of anyone else. All who listened to his music, heard his passionate plea to follow Jesus radically, or watched the international rise of Last Days Ministries (LDM), which Keith and his wife Melody began, will tell you of the immense and ongoing impact he made.

Keith was unique. How many of us know a young man who begins a journal of his life at age 15 and keeps it for the next 13 years? Keith's journal entries are often sporadic, but they cover all of his life, ending less than a week before his death. On July 28, 1982, Keith's earthly life ended at age 28. Two of his children died with him—Josiah three, and Bethany, two. Melody was home with one-year-old Rebekah, and six weeks pregnant with their fourth child, Rachel.

Keith's death was a tragedy of huge proportions, and the Christian community worldwide grieved openly. But by the grace of God, Keith's voice still continues to be heard 20 years after his death.

Many of the selections from Keith's journals are published here for the very first time. Selections from his concert messages are here in print for the first time, too. Through both we get a more complete picture of Keith Green than ever before. In his journals, we meet a man who loved Jesus with deep intensity, yet was often frustrated by the lack of personal discipline and Christian growth he saw in his own life. In his concert messages, we hear the public Keith Green exhorting us to live wholly for God, no matter what the cost. Both sides of Keith's life are true. Both are genuine.

You'll soon discover Keith's struggles were very much the same ones we all face. Like us, Keith had his successes...and his failures. Like us, Keith exercised good judgment...and he made mistakes. But through it all, we see God at work moving a man toward his final destiny—heaven.

And when Keith reached that destination, the world wasn't ready to lose him. Those of us who had been touched by him were stunned and heartbroken. But when we heard Melody, his young pregnant widow, quote John 12:24, we knew the words were true: "Unless a grain of wheat falls into the earth and dies, it remains alone; but if it dies, it bears much fruit" (NASB).

Since Keith's homegoing we *have* seen the "much fruit." Keith's music and writings still speak to believers and unbelievers alike. The testimony of his life still reaches readers through Melody's bestselling and often translated biography, *No Compromise: The Life Story of Keith Green*. In a second book called *If You Love the Lord: Uncompromising Devotions from the Heart of Keith Green*, the challenging words from some of the hundreds of Bible studies taught still inspire us to live passionately for God. His powerful music coupled with his passionate delivery continues to travel throughout the world, touching hearts and changing the lives of people of all ages.

Most recently, Keith is serving God through a new medium he never anticipated. Melody has taken Keith's writings and music—all the Last Days Ministries classics—as well as her own ministry, onto the information super highway now known as cyberspace—a word that didn't exist in Keith's time. At the Web sites www.KeithGreen.com or www.MelodyGreen.com Melody continues to spread the music, the messages, and her ever-growing vision to reach the world—a message Jesus first put into her and Keith's hearts many years ago.

And yet for all this attention to Keith Green the man, Keith would be the first to shrug his shoulders and say he lived his life to glorify Jesus Christ, not Keith Green. In his concerts Keith was openly upset if people got more excited about him than about Jesus. So the message of this book isn't meant to be so much about Keith himself, but about how God worked in the life of someone who finally and totally yielded to Him. It is about Keith's desire for greater intimacy with God, his love for his wife and children, and his desire to be used by God in humility and integrity.

God has a plan for each of us, no less important than the one He had for Keith. Much remains to be done in the Kingdom, and Jesus is still calling for willing, abandoned servants who are intent on glorifying God with their lives.

As we read Keith's words from his personal journals and his exhortations from the concert messages, may we be challenged to the same depth of commitment Keith made. And as we read of Keith's struggles—the same struggles we all face, if we're honest with ourselves—may we realize that God desires to use each of us, even in our imperfection. We just need to let Him do it.

May God make each of our lives a prayer!

Harvest House Publishers
October 2001

A Word from Melody About the Journals

My husband Keith lived only 28 years on earth. Of those years, 21 were spent searching for spiritual truth. After reading his personal journals and seeing his relentless, gut-wrenching search for God, you'll better understand why Keith was so intense about sharing his faith with others. After all, he fought so long and hard to find those answers himself.

I met Keith when he was 18. He sat me down, for the first of many times, and read his journals to me—out loud and unedited. He wanted me to *really* know him—the good, the bad, and the unlovely. If Keith was anything, he was honest—with himself and with others. I totally loved him for that. His early journal entries talk about running away from home (three times!), high school problems, music, girls, his parents, fear of going to war, and his best friend, Todd Fishkind.

In his journals, Keith asked honest questions about real life. I am always shaken when I see his unquenchable hunger for truth and his total abandonment to finding it. When Keith was just 17 he desperately wrote, *"God help me! I'll ask a million times. I'll try forever!"* Just days ago this entry brought me to tears. How could God *not* respond to this kind of prayer?

Keith's journals are important for many reasons. One is because they paint an honest portrait. These journals allow Keith to speak for himself in a candid and often surprising way. Keith always wrote and spoke openly about himself. I can say with certainty that Keith would be deeply offended if anyone tried to present a perfect picture of him, now that he is with Jesus. Still, Keith Green was one of the greatest men of God I've ever known. He walked in integrity, strove for authenticity, and was honest and very real.

Keith read the Bible, believed it, and acted on it. Some felt that the lines he drew were too hard. Others had been waiting a long time for someone like Keith to show up and tell it like it was. But Keith's urgency came from deep within. He knew how it felt to plead with God and not really *know* Him—to finally find the truth, become a minister, and then struggle to live up to his own message.

Keith gathered manna each day, but it was never enough for the next. He always wanted *more*. He struggled to keep his integrity and a good conscience, to have Holy Spirit anointing, consistent prayer, personal discipline—and he fought his own bad attitudes. And contrary to what some thought, Keith *did* understand the truth of God's grace. In fact, the more Keith struggled, the more he discovered and enjoyed the unmerited mercy of God.

Keith made an impact on people that most men would give their whole life to achieve. Funny thing is, Keith didn't really care about achieving it. He just wanted to please Jesus. Yes, he did want to change the world—but he wanted God to get all the glory for it. Keith was terrified of ever, even accidentally, touching God's glory. Perhaps that's why God allowed him to accomplish so much, in so little time. Keith made an indelible impact on a whole generation—an impact that continues to be made today on a brand-new generation around the world.

One night Keith told me I could do something with his journals if anything ever happened to him. He added with a smile, "Edited, of course…" Some editing was needed for length, clarity, or privacy, but I've never changed the meaning or intent of any entry. In most cases, I've also allowed Keith's punctuation, grammar, underlining, and capitalization to remain just as he wrote it—from the heart.

I now invite you to get to know a more intimate side of Keith Green. Perhaps you'll be most touched by his vulnerability. But you'll also see his longing that the church would rise up and *be* the church—be the jewel she is. You'll see his genuine love for people, his desire for lost souls to find their Maker, and his deep compassion for those who are hurting. These are the things that pierced his heart—just as they should ours.

Sometimes I wonder how Keith could not have known that his life *really was* a prayer.

Melody Green
October 2001

The Journals

1969–1982

1969–1970

July 8, 1969 [age 15]

Sorry about the messy writing. We're driving. Hi there. My name is Keith Green. I'm splitting Canoga Park. Our final goal is Canada! We've been planning to leave for two months. We have luggage, organ and amplifier, $175.39 and my coin collection worth about $100. I hope to get some jobs along the coast of California singing and playing. We're going as far from L.A. as we can.

I really feel sorry about my parents. I love them. They're goin' to feel bad. —Later.

October 25, 1970, 4 PM, Home

Me and [my friend] Todd are musicians and songwriters and children of God. (As everyone is.) We feel we have been placed together for a reason—to help the Peaceful Revolutionary Movement!

October 28, 1970, 9:30 AM

Our dream is to have a big musical family, sort of like a communal living type thing. We'd like to grow our own fruits and vegetables. So I told Todd if he wants to start getting into the commune living type life, to stop taking vitamins, because we can't grow them.

December 10, 1970, 12:45 AM, Seattle, WA

We went to a "Jesus Freak" coffeehouse and they tried to trip on me about believing the whole Bible, word for word, even the part that says God kills my brother and I just don't believe that. Not my wonderful Father!

1971

New Year's Day, 1971, Seattle, WA

I've decided to put down dope. All phases of it. Grass, psychics, whatever. I'm holding my sex in check too. I'm really growing but words are useless. I have to prove it with actions.

March 4, 1971, 6:15 PM

I pray constantly. But I'd like to write one more written prayer.

"Father: tomorrow let us reflect all *your* wondrous beauty. All your perfect rhythm and all your limitless brotherhood. Thank you."

March 19, 1971, 3:30 PM

…God, please help us get *your* music to *your* children.

March 23, 1971

I think it would be a beautiful thing someday to live…on a farm and have some children. I have so much to teach children and I bet they have much to teach me. I really have a lot of growth left until I reach heaven (state of mind).

I have been really aware lately of how I treat people. I pray every day to love everyone equally. God has been helping lately. We don't want to be Joe and Jerry Judge! We need to express more compassion to our brothers in the pit, "judge for the sake of helping, not for condemning!"

March 25, 1971

I just tasted a banana for the first time. I didn't like it, but I might be able to get into it. It takes time. Todd turned me onto apples and oranges too. Now I eat them all the time.

Today I had so much inner struggle inside me that I had to write something, so I wrote this: It says it all. My emotions. This is a piece called:

Inner Peace

When the "Dark Age" began,
    I knew that I'd feel this way, someday;
Someday is here
    and I can't put my finger on the feeling.
All I know is the <u>inner peace</u> I've found
    is slipping away.
It might be a <u>test</u> but it's slipping away…
I want to give love, to express peace,
    to be good and <u>give</u>…
These things I've done, but not with a light heart.
I've been measuring my good deeds.
"To give <u>without</u> measure," The Moody Blues
    write.
I've got to express <u>endless</u> good, and that's right.
You must recognize the darkness before you can
    turn on the light.
INNER PEACE IS STILL THERE, always.
BROTHERHOOD!?!
People <u>screaming</u> brotherhood!
I feel ashamed sometimes when they
    use that word.
Throwing words and rocks and bottles at their
    brothers that they deny!
Brothers? Yes! I give them that.
But not expressing brotherhood.

Sometimes I feel myself captured by the
   animal inside.
Coming out, hatefully, gnashing its teeth, and
   clawing at my brothers.
Sometimes I hate myself. But is it really me?

March 27, 1971, 11:35 PM
   I'm listening to John Lennon's album. He's really good.

March 29, 1971, 12:05 PM
   Today me <u>and</u> Todd got kicked out of our boring
Humanities class because we were acting immature. That was
kind of deserved. But right now it doesn't feel like punish-
ment to be out of school because we're going swimming. We
found out today about a rock festival in Death Valley, like a
Woodstock West. So if we don't go to Washington we have
something to fall back on.
   I don't know where my right place is supposed to be, but
God does.

March 30, 1971
   My father didn't wake me up today to go to school. He is
disgusted with his bearded, long hair, revolutionary son. I went
to the bank and withdrew $63 in case they throw me out. On
the way here I stopped into a beautiful, spacious Catholic
church and prayed. They had candles there that you can light
for 10 cents donation, for yourself to God. I lit two, one for me
and one for bro' Todd. Later.

7:50 PM
   My parents are confused about what's real.

April 12, 1971, 1:30 PM

We are back in that deep rut of school again! It feels like there never was a vacation, although I feel somewhat rested. There are so many things that are in God's hands. School, recording, the draft, and on into the future, but I shouldn't worry. So what else is new?

A COMPOSITION KEITH WROTE
FOR ENGLISH CLASS

I met the young Indian, Jakilma, on a warm August afternoon in a border town near San Antone, Texas. His face was ageless, with the youth of spring and the lines of centuries. His hair was flowing down his shoulders and the breeze made it look like a cool running stream. He came to me with a knowing smile and asked in a tone that accented timelessness, "You are Pablo?"

I asked, "How did you know?" I was very surprised, but took warm comfort in his smile. Somehow, somewhere I had seen this man; met this man. For I felt as if I had known him forever!

He said, "I know. I know all brothers." His confidence was not surprising, looking into his eyes. He said, "Come, we have a long way to go."

He started walking, and I followed without question, motivated by some strange force within. It didn't feel evil, but somehow fulfilling. Whenever I felt tired, I looked into his always brilliant eyes and was filled with the stamina to endure almost anything. When I felt thirsty, I drank, at first conservatively. My canteen emptied the first day. There was no water anywhere in sight. But Jakilma's canteen seemed always full. We drank a lot but there was always more. When I asked him of this, he said, "Faith is my food and drink."

I understood.

April 15, 1971, 2:20 PM

I'm never perfect while I'm on earth. (Well, it's improbable but I guess not impossible.) We had an earthquake today at 3 AM. It woke most everybody up. During earthquakes you feel so helpless, like you're in a little rowboat in the middle of a rough ocean, tossed all about. All you can do is pray and pray some more.

April 23, 1971

I'm finishing up <u>Demian</u> by Hesse. Demian believes in a God that encompasses both good and evil. All things, not just the good. I am on the side of good, because it is the real powerful, eternal thing. Evil is a fooling illusion, only there to sway us. Part of the game. The devil is the Good-Humor man.

May 3, 1971

Hassles with my parents do not cease.

I felt the presence of God's protection last night. I went up to Box Canyon to visit brother Dimples who wasn't home and as I was driving down it began to rain. The road became very slippery and I went into a skid. The car was spinning around and also going down the road at 40 miles an hour. There was 20 feet between the mountain and fence. I yelled out to God, and the car gently came to rest on the fence. <u>No</u> damage. I felt God's hand protecting me.

Today is good. I need help with relationships.

1:45 PM

I feel so discontent today, I feel unfulfilled. Searching for something to quench my thirst for fulfillment. I wrote a letter to sister Joni Mitchell but haven't mailed it yet. An orange plant came up yesterday. I gave Todd and Allyn and Jay apple plants Sunday.

Searching—loving peacefully, everybody's brother, Keith.

May 14, 1971

Theories

In my youth I go through many changes and many different beliefs. I find that sometimes one year contradicts another. It's very enjoyable and also very confusing. But as each year goes by, there seems to be a clear defined path, a sort of "road of life."

When I was very young, I went to Sunday School. I hated going to Sunday School. But of course my parents knew what was right, so they gently <u>forced</u> me to go. I (not-so-gently) rebelled against all religious beliefs because of my being forced to go to Sunday School. I didn't believe in God, or love, or brotherhood. I was a materialist in its youngster form!

Then as I got older, started talking to my friends, and feeling the spirit within me, I developed a belief (based on Christian Science, in which I was raised) that <u>only</u> spirit was real: that all material, all physicalities were an illusion, a dream I was having, not reality. Well I made a fool of myself, strangling my friends with wisdom.

As time went on, I found that I was not at peace with my immovable position on matter and material things not being real. There were so many things around me that were beautiful, that I felt I could no longer deny reality.

Then I found Hermann Hesse…I read <u>Demian</u> in which Demian believes in a god called Abraxas who engulfs <u>both</u> good and evil, material and spirit, *all* opposites! This I didn't accept until I read <u>Siddhartha</u>. Siddhartha was a man who first believed in spirit only, then material only and accepted all things, everything as having its place in the hand of fate, also in the unity of the universe.

I now agree with this last concept for I feel much more at peace with it. And it makes sense (at least as long as I live on this plane). Things now are less complicated, and I can trace the cycles behind all happenings through history and my life. I feel I have taken a step <u>forward</u>.

I will not hold firmly to this belief because of all the changes I have already been through. There might be more (inevitably). So I must travel this "road" with an open mind.

"I've got to admit it's getting better, a little better all the time"—Beatles, 1967   —Brother Keith '71

May 17, 1971, 11:05 AM

Todd and I are differing much lately, but I'm not going to let it affect our relationship. We are drawing our own conclusions. Someday the (New Dawn) (the mystery) truth will be revealed and all misconceptions destroyed. And I have many (undoubtedly).

Todd and most people hate the idea of maybe being a tool for destiny (God), or as Todd calls it a puppet, but even as an old hermit in a dark cave hates the sun, it doesn't stop shining or existing. If destiny does rule our life completely, no matter how much people hate the idea, it still would be a true reality.

Personally, I don't mind being a tool. After all, I am a unique tool that takes part in doing the job I'm meant to do.

June 1, 1971

I have found that if you keep feelings out of a close relationship, you lose closeness and respect for each other's presence and love.

June 24, 1971

[While hitchhiking north, Keith was picked up by some people who went to a ballet. Keith went along because he didn't want to be stuck alone in San Francisco. Afterwards he went to a coffeehouse on the North Shore.]

There was a piano there and I was frantic because I wanted to play. Most of the people were drunk there, but I had such an urge to play, such energy that wanted to shine. Well, I got on and played that pian'er and I showed it no mercy. I beat it to death and the crowd roared after each song. It was wonderful. So fulfilling.

June 26, 1971

1. The <u>peaceful</u> revolution. If we cannot bring about the revolution (or change) without judging, drawing sides, and prejudice, then there will be another revolution when we become the establishment. For if we don't try and change this world differently than others have tried before, we will have accomplished nothing new, nothing permanent.

2. I hear you shout "peace," and then I hear the bombs explode. Who are you trying to kill? What are you trying to kill? Is it something inside of you?

3. You will oppress others if you accept only those who believe as you do. We cannot deny any person. We must accept everyone, even if they don't accept us. And we must make this part of our goal.

4. We will achieve, for we cannot draw lines. Everyone is on the side of humanity.

5. There's gonna be a peaceful revolution when everyone realizes the truth. The power is in the youth. Real youth is mental.

6. The power is to the children and a child is anyone who can accept. "Acceptance" is a key word to peace on earth and brotherhood among all. (I am not perfect and don't profess to be, but I realize my goal.) I am striving for it, and I hope in the music you find a glimpse of yours, and together someday we will reach the Common Goal.

I am with you. Be happy. Your brother, Keith.

July 5, 1971, 1:30 PM

I'm at brother Todd's. We are listening to JC Superstar. It's great.

Sunday I stayed home and started reading a Modern Day translation of the Bible. I read the complete book of Matthew. It was really a mind blower. It scared me a little. I don't know what to think. There's so much confusion in knowledge. Sometimes I wonder if I have unearthed any wisdom at all! I don't know anymore. I'm searching and waiting patiently.

This week I try again to break the barrier in recording. Something sure doesn't want it recorded. At least now I need the Creator's help. He created it, and now He must help it get through to His children.

Hey, I love you God!

July 6, 1971

Last night I brought home from Todd's some tapes. Joni Mitchell, Chicago, Procol Harum, and Crosby. It's good to get into other people's music. I've got to get those new albums.

July 7, 1971

Today is traffic court and a test in government. Tomorrow, God willing, we will finally get the ball rolling. I'm supposed to meet with a producer. It's His show anyway. "God, Thy will is hard; but you hold <u>every</u> card!" That's a line from JC Superstar, a trip.

Later:

In traffic court I got my license suspended for two weeks. He gave me a choice of a $25 fine or two weeks suspension and I took the latter. The appointment with the producer got put forward. God do it!

August 1, 1971, 11:30 PM

Today is a great day. School is leaving me behind. Thank my daddy-God! I realized tonight that Jesus and God are one, for Jesus ascended into the great universal soul, so he became one with it, and when you pray to Jesus, you are praying to God and all that He encompasses.

August 11, 1971, 2:15 AM

These are in-between times—a transition period between two major parts of life.

1. childhood—education, dependency on parents.
2. manhood—learning, shining, doing our life's work.

I graduated Friday with no ceremonies or fireworks. Getting drunk was a drag. Also the movies. But I met a most beautiful sister...

I wish I knew how to control myself. Most of the time I don't know how I work. I'm lost without God—praying.

August 14, 1971, 2:10 PM

A good, good trip. I flipped out. And I learned about ego and I killed part of my false ego. But I know that acid is not my Savior. Everybody is me. Everything is me.

Wisdom is being able to accept the flow of all good and evil, both in the stream. It will be hard, so hard, to stay here. I want to flow, be harmonious with everyone in this universe. The key to this is to look at anyone as yourself. You have to love everyone as yourself, because they are. I could write for hours. But it's all here. Good life.

October 22, 1971

Back here in the "together diary" I am now a free, legal, 18-year-old, as of yesterday. I received a most beautiful gift from my family. A combination graduation/birthday present.

December 15, 1971

[Keith thinks he's losing Todd's friendship.]

We have previous commitments to fill out and after that maybe he'll find he can't hack me, or something. I can't hack me most of the time, but I'm stuck with me, so I've got to like myself or have a miserable life. To change myself for the better, I'm definitely searching for. I've tried to change and it's futile. That doesn't mean I'm giving up, but I'm praying for help more than I ever have.

Randy [Wimer] from [the band] MU once told me "as long as you cry out to God, evil can't lead you wrong." I sure need help, and Todd said to me in Seattle, "We need each other so much, we can't do it alone." Unity is the key, unity is the key.

Maybe the Rosicrucian Order is the answer.

I'd like to join with you [Todd] in the new house. You tell me about you wasting your precious time, I understand completely 'cause me too, yeah, me too.

But our time will continue to be futilely wasted until we direct our growing energies toward each other. We've been placed together and we both know our differences and we both realize many similarities, but not that many. There's many more to discover.

What I am trying to say is we are each other's right path.

December 9, 1971, 3 AM

I came home [from a party] and fell asleep reading the new translations of Revelation in the Bible. I awoke at 1:30 AM and had a sandwich and watched a monster movie with my mom. I finished Revelation and now I can't fall asleep.

December 24, 1971

Christmas Eve was spent wrapping presents and the usual family trips. Exchanging giftless gifts. Later, with friends coccaine rained.

December 26, 1971, 5:20 AM

Well, Xmas has come and gone. At Todd's—tripping. Me and Todd are forever closer. I'm improving. New year's a' coming. I am still searching. Always.

1972

January 1, 1972

Lately (last two days) I've felt myself slip down to normal again. Hateful—argumentative—and a judge and a half. God is a protective veil encircling me. One thing I'm looking forward to is college.

I also got a money order for six months Rosicrucian dues.

February 2, 1972

An old friend told me that the 1973 draft lottery was today. I called the Times office and heard the great news. Todd's number is 294 and mine is 288 and Jimmy's is 257. The highest number they pick is 150 usually. We are free from that strangling draft. God thank you.

February 9, 1972

Wednesday we went to school and it's beginning to feel like school. Work!?! I'm such a spoiled, lazy ass that even the slightest school vibes bug me. It's much easier for Todd anyway at school because he's been used to a much harder routine. Me—lazy!

March 16, 1972

I am in such a struggle. Animal/brother. God help me! I'll ask a million times. I'll try forever.

March 17, 1972

I've been thinking very strongly on my loose moral code. There's many things I do that hurt other people. There are many things I do that hurt myself. I've got to make a <u>straight</u> attempt to change.

These are the goals I want to obtain:

1. to act like brother Keith.

2. to not have any sex outside of love.

3. to not depend on dope for happiness, and eventually to remain straight continually.

4. to not eat a lot of junk food, like sundaes and candy and other things.

These goals are hard.

The hardest is number one. I have done the other three for a short while. I have many fasts to do, "to act like brother Keith" is a responsibility I must fulfill. I will try today, then again tomorrow. Jesus, I ask for your help.

March 19, 1972

Today we got up early, and went to a lecture in Hollywood with friends about the prophecies found in the pyramids. Outrageous.

March 20, 1972, 1:30 PM

Spring has sprung, the grass has riz.
And I know where the flowers is.
God bless us onward, bye to winter '72
And old trips therein.

March 25, 1972

Today is washing day. My hair, my car, and the house. I pray for my soul too. Ha.

June 1, 1972

Lately I've been struggling (to say the least), purging the blackness from my being. Reading the biblical novel that I'm reading is boggling my mind down with creeds and trips from the Bible and the author and my previous beliefs. I am spinning around dizzily, and in the process becoming a very messed person to be around.

My brethren are being very compassionate, which I cannot express enough or any gratitude for. It seems dumb, but I am so very withdrawn lately. I am rejecting all and everyone.

God (I cry to God whom I don't know practically anything about—blind faith) help!!! Thank you Lord, your humble son and slave and curious seeker.

There's this force inside me that is so selfish it makes me cringe. It wants all the ladies. And forget all else. It wants all good things and forget everyone else. I see this force and don't want to be near anyone…write any music or be nice because I am afraid this force will show itself.

I don't care about loneliness anymore. I want to be good. To shine. I've never prayed with such conviction. Beyond all else, God whatever you are, help us to unite in harmony without greed, lust, and selfishness.

June 4, 1972

Who knows what the day holds. Help me through the temptations and struggles, God.

What a torture this past week has been. Oh, it has been horrible. God show me something to lift my burden off my back. Help!

August 9, 1972

Continued transition between boy and man. I see others growing into the boy I was, and some boys starting out as the man I hope to be. I am feeling different every day. Getting older and younger. "You have to go to your roots to grow larger."

I really feel like crying. I'm really scared, really scared of all this future. I need a booster shot—no, a continual flow of faith and energy and reassurance. I see this is gonna be some roller-coaster ride. Help! This feeling is new.

September 20, 1972

Awoke resting, reading, writing, and warming up. At 3:30—sound, and lights at the hall. At 8:15—concert. What can I say, but "You are the power and glory forever."

I am so very far from living that attitude. It only comes up like sparsely populated flowers in a field of weeds. Lord, you are the Master Gardener. Burn my weeds and help the flowers grow. Make me balanced.

October 11, 1972

While I slept, things ironed out inside, and somehow I didn't feel too bad. And today I felt that I <u>could</u> cope with the heavy future. At least near future. Prayers seemed to work.

I got my license renewed for 4 years. Didn't study at all for the test. Prayed a lot and got no mistakes. Prayers seemed to work.

I think things are improving but confusion still has control.

October 28, 1972

Tomorrow is free. I have a gig on November 5th at the Riverside Cafe.

Poem:
Towers of happiness
built on the sand of confusion
usually tumble down.
I'm digging deep, I'm digging deep,
gotta find that solid rock foundation.

I'm digging deep, I'm washing with water
and cleansing in soil.
When I reach a solid self, if there is [one]
then I'll build a cabin of home in my heart.
And maybe share it with another solid soul.
Bless the growing world.

December 16, 1972

Jesus, you are hereby officially welcomed into me. Now only action will reveal your effect on me.

December 31, 1972

<u>Gotta Find a Home</u>

My roots dangle. Unnourished, I refuse to root here! Gotta find a home and get it settled and peaceful. Gotta find a place inside where I can rest between crises...

Please, Jesus! I know you more each day and recognize the signs you show me. The immaculate birth makes you special above all men and strengthens all the links to the Christian trip—keep the signs coming. I'd almost given myself up for lost. Bless you. Beloved clean brother on highest.

1973

January 3, 1973

I am amazed at how unimproved I am over three years. All that's changed is that I am more aware of the false problems and sins than before. BUT: I continue wasting away, show me. If there's help—

January 11, 1973

My fear lately consists of not being afraid. I wonder if this is not just trying to get me off my guard. Taking my mind off the things I'm fearful of. Sin—hell—self-destruction—and death, and even disease. Ignoring it won't help. I just feel more at ease and it seems right for now. But I wonder if the old saying applies, "Give 'em enough rope (freedom from fear) and he'll hang himself!"

Help me Jesus!

January 15, 1973

Spiritually, I'm still very baffled. I'm learning to love Jesus.

Am I looking for a perfect one for me? I must work on perfecting myself! The more perfect I become, the less I judge and categorize people, and the more I can see through shallow trips, like looks and age and all those other "simple on paper changes in outlook, but difficult to practice" things. God—Father—Jesus, help me help myself!

January 17, 1973

Called Randy Stonehill. I may see him tomorrow, but we're for sure gonna write on Thursday.

The situation here is getting rough. I gotta move out soon. My parents are getting truly fed up with me, with much right. I've got to change some basic things in my self.

These spiritual daily summaries are the hardest yet. The most important part of my entries.

I've been questioning the righteousness of sex in my heart. I know for a fact that sex without love is dead wrong. Now my use of the word "love" has a changeable definition. I know it has changed extremely the past four years. (Or has it? Have I become more cynical and does it take "love" longer to break through and reach me?) At any rate, love has been a different, deeper thing for me. At least I am more careful.

Anyway, sex with love rings true in me. If it is wrong out of marriage—or even in marriage for recreation (against procreation), let it be shown to me—please be my guide!

Goals for near future:

Find a nice home either with someone or alone, but comfortable.

Finish all unfinished songs.

Continue tape for new songs.

Be good and seek purity. Keep clean.

January 19, 1973

I am drawn to the Christian trip more and more, but hypocrisy lurks all around. I feel very swayable and maneuverable now. Christ, guide me and protect.

January 20, 1973

I feel a crisis point coming where I will throw off many shackles. It's time to stand up against the undercurrent! God help me and be with me. I am grateful.

January 26, 1973

Sexual Dilemma and Other Relations

Gotta break the habit of how I relate to women. Even more so, I've got to break my way of unconsciously relating with people—not realizing how incredibly complex and simple and fascinating and unique and incredibly miraculous and interesting each and every one is! Gotta listen and observe and learn.

January 27, 1973

Pride is the big pitfall. It makes you stop working. These changes are the start of new work on my relating self. Help me help myself.

January 28, 1973

Poem: <u>Staying Conscious</u>

Staying conscious is like holding out your arms for an
hour, then realizing you've got to hold them out
for a year (at least) more—
It is like conquering a problem in Algebra
then continuing to Calculus and beyond,
immediately being tested after each correct answer.
It is my goal.
It is my hope and peace of spirit. It is my purpose here.

January 30, 1973

Poem: <u>Every Day I Start Over New</u>

To swim in guilt and self-punishment
is as time-wasting as not seeing your mistakes.
Self-discipline is absolutely necessary
to master one's self, but every day I start over new.
Each day I start out with a clean record
so I can travel lighter without guilty afflictions,
or pride-laden medals of victory (for small battles).
The war with one's self never ends,
'cause the enemy is subtle in thinking that peace,
humanly, is won eternally...

January 31, 1973

Wrote a song. I feel stronger, reimbursed. I can write!! I can write!! It isn't all over for me—I'm still inspired!! The sun shines in my window again. Thank you Father.

February 1, 1973, 2:00 AM
[Reflecting back on the 31st]

Awoke to mom/dog hassles. Went to Matrix Image and rapped with Richard—still positive, but gotta watch out about overconfidence.

Talked to Melody, the secretary there—I'm attracted to her—she's a musician-writer-singer-creator. Very changing lady. Attracted.

February 5, 1973
<u>Shadow Ranch Park</u>

Things blew up at my house. Before and inside me. My father told me tonight was my last night there. All my judgments of myself hit me at once, and I packed everything. I cried better than I have in years. Resentment and spite evolved to disgust in myself. My mother begged me not to leave tonight, but I didn't want to put off facing myself. I left and cried in torrents. So cleansing. Was led here to Shadow Ranch Park and prayed. I am here in bed in my van Barney with my dog Libre. I feel more peace.

February 13, 1973

...I hope someone's watching over me.
I need a parent-spirit.
We all do.

February 13, 1973

Poem: "So Nice to Have a Friend"

It's so nice not to have to be anyone else but me.
Because you like me—my friend.
As I am—my friend.
It's so nice to have someone to cry to.
And be spontaneously, bitingly honest and open—
or moody with—you understand—my friend.
Do you exist elsewhere besides in my mind?
You don't ask me to be to you what you are to me.
That makes me want to try to be there for you.
When people don't ask me to give to them,
it makes me want to.

February 14, 1973

Is Success a Curse?

When I'm comfy and stuffed and earthly satisfied, will my innocence be stomped dead and buried?

February 27, 1973

Tortured celibacy, self-discipline. Look, the root of discipline is disciple. I've been far away from any religious trips or beliefs. I really like believing. I love it. It's people's faith that gives them beauty.

Boy, do I feel old. I wanna be reborn, I want to be clean. I wanna be free. I want what God wants. Or does God know us?

March 2, 1973

Poem: "Beginning of March"

The beginning of March
finds me not trusting any person,

And my faith light needs fuel badly.
God is a distant thought.
I am truly in the depth of night.
But experience tells me that the sun will rise again.
I hope sometime I will be worthy
of getting out of these cycles.
For I already look ahead
to high noon fearing the fall of night.
Fear is my worst enemy, it eats me away.

Gonna remain open and listen for God to reach me. Gonna seek and search and travel and try to grow. Gonna play and write spring music, (and if I may excuse myself) GOD'S MUSIC.

March 7, 1973
[At a table in the cafeteria at Western Washington College, Bellingham]

Here I sit about two-and-one-third years after first writing here (almost 3 years since I first came to this city). Ladies don't have the same magic as they used to, but neither do I have the same naivety, or susceptibility to their magic.

I am old and senile at 19.

But they still make me turn my head…and (at least) begin to pursue them.

But my heart isn't in it, just like in Santa Barbara in February. My heart seeks an understanding on how I can be a thing called righteous, and how I can begin to perceive a thing called eternal/and God, the most variable word (like "x" in algebra) I know of.

When you're young, your ideals are strong—then you yourself are the least liver of them and you suddenly quiet your protest down to a whisper. Until either you are broken; or you have the strength to be able to endure long-suffering. At that point I believe a thing tagged wisdom is attained and either you remain silent, or speak simply and quietly. Equals righteously.

March 8, 1973

Listened to records and wrote a good poem.

The Christ decision is on my head. Is Christ a big, non-individual-spiritual-plane? Or a being who is Lord over us—under Father—infinity God?? My mind reels when I think of the meaning of such words.

Tomorrow Baba Ram Dass speaks at Mt. Vernon.

March 10, 1973

Here I am with the wonderful dog Banana again. Seattle today. L.A. tonight or tomorrow. Oh what can I say? These spiritual parts can be torture. I am dirty inside. I hate myself a lot. Tonight I feared losing my personal guiding angel inside—I felt it leaving me, after I played. But this is probably only a weird fantasy. I need an answer so bad. What and where is God, and who am I?

May 8, 1973

Poem: "May"

And May finds me in love with Melody.

Writing a bit.

And working a little at getting a song placed.

I got a new car and I stay at Mel's a lot and

I'm working at Dirty Pierre's tonight.

On the horizon looms the north trip
in two and a half weeks.
Also Christ is a very fond thought indeed.
My body is near a nice place.
My mind needs control.

June 27, 1973

Poem: "Dying"
Today is death
Tomorrow is birth
Show myself
What I am worth
I want to die
A symbolic death
Birth
Rebirth
Nothing new, everything that would seem new
is already dead or dying.

September 20, 1973

Bless our autumn, make us know you more fully and through
you know ourselves and each other with humility and compassion. God bless you Master Jesus. Save us.

September 24, 1973

Poem: "Up to Now"
I haven't been faithful to my poetry book.
I kept a lot inside myself so no one could look.
At my tumultuous struggle and my ugly self.
At times I've misplaced this book
At other times I've hidden it.

I have to tell it everything
I have to bare my soul to it
It never offers condolence
Only stares me back
And eats as many words as I will feed it

"Love—Melody—Love"

My youth washes away (I guess). And Melody, oh bless her! Stays constant in reciprocal love—my music is blooming again. Wow it's really been a long time!! We weren't even in this house then, we weren't engaged. We've been to New York. MCA Records is a positive place for me. So much, so much.

We have a new dog. We are to be married on Christmas with the Lord's blessings. We are now into the used and home-made clothing business. We thrift shop. Mel sews and we sell clothes on an empty lot in Hollywood. We are becoming more and more Christians everyday. I accept Jesus Christ as my personal Savior and put Him first in my life.

December 24, 1973

We got our marriage license and our rings. Ate at the health food store and record shopped. Visited parents and Todd came home with us. We played cards and crashed.

December 31, 1973

So ends another chapter of this diary in my life. On Xmas day of 1973, I married Melody and it has changed my life. God, thank you for this and all other blessings you bestow upon your children. I pray for continued vision of your plan in the name of Jesus Christ our Lord.

1974

March 20, 1974

Through this whole period in my life, I have been silently alarmed by my distance from God, but signs continue to peer in the music and I also fully realize that Melody is a divine gift and that she's helped me grow and grow. Been reading the Bible a bit lately, especially James. The only book that I fully agree with. Anyway, there is so much that is lost time erosion, here is the end of winter, 1974.

Spring 1974
I feel so murky.
Like a glass of water that had a drop or two
of milk at the bottom.
The glass is my life.
The water is spring.
The milk is time and its mind-numbing effect.
My Melody writes a happy ode to spring.
I breathe in and out and
wish only for the bliss of childhood.
Poems are like leaves.
They grow old and die.
Lose life and meaning.
Life is the tree.
God is the life.
I am the branch.
My body and finite thought are the leaves.
I'm sorry to treat spring so restlessly.
I am sad only because I know too much of human life.
God bless us.

Make us blissful.
Children of you, God.
I still believe in God.

June 5, 1974

I've learned that I have to harness my energy more consciously. The key word is <u>consciousness</u>. Clear, humble, non-drugged, non-self-centered thinking. God bless my striving towards this goal.

July 29, 1974

<u>God</u>

There is no one to talk about how I feel. I love the Christ always—and Jesus and all the words and works.

There's metaphysical Christians—and there's Jesus Freaks that scream, yell, and chant His name, but there's no confused Christians like me—that I can see or meet.

I love the goal so thoroughly that I'd give up anything to attain it if I were sure about the path.

I believe in the virgin birth, all the miracles, and the ascension, but I don't want to just do lip service. (But I do see the value in speaking the truth—including names and credit where it is due to the Master, or/and God.)

And metaphysics is so dry and so indigestible to my spiritual heart.

Ah! My heart—

It wants to break for the truth and its fulfilling substance.

It is time to put away diversions and time-wasting-fillers—and seek the truth and speak the truth and love my neighbor, truly love them all. Harness my tongue and mind. Point my every day in God's direction for His service only, only, only, only, not mine!

November 24, 1974

Poem: <u>Melody</u>

My sister Melody is my fullest blessing in my life.
She fulfills every quality
of the seldom treasured word, wife.
In Christ's name we joined our earthly life together.
And now in God's sight I swear to comfort her whole life
and try to bring her the joy she endlessly gives me.
I praise you God, you knew my needs and
you know ours now. I entrust my life to you.
I feel like singing psalms of praises over and over to you. I
pray that my deeds to come will be psalms of praise to you.
I know <u>You</u> have changed <u>me</u>.

November 25, 1974

<u>Turmoil</u>

I feel less than well now, but rejoice in knowing that I'm choosing God as my world. Evil has had a field trip in my life, pulling me here and there, and has me pulled away by surprise, and it's not giving up without a fight.

Praise You God for You are doing the fighting with evil for me. I have and am resisting the devil and he will and is fleeing from me.

On the way home I was feeling high, and made a resolution to accept Jesus as my Savior, after much, much struggling and questioning—I got a very beautiful peace all through me. When I got home I wanted to tell Melody and she had a lot to share with me.

Anyway, I immediately proceed to tell her about my accepting Jesus as my personal Savior, and all my doubts came out, and dethroned my assurance. So there I was, totally lost and feeling empty. And Melody started to tell me about her happy growings all day and I couldn't listen. And Melody closed up, and I tried to pry her open and she wouldn't, and we both got emotional. I reacted irrationally and even played some ugly fight games.

Later on we both came around and I found myself crying, and feeling extremely sorry I had lowered into an ugly part of me (a lie). (God is even now loosening parts of me that aren't really me, they only claim to be, and as they drift out of me, they make it clear that they don't like going.) Melody forgave me and we went on with the day. Her writing, my reading, and praying for a Savior answer.

November 26, 1974

<u>Tears and Lessons</u>

Learning my lessons from many falls. I do not want to offend the Lord. I cried twice today, for I shamed myself in the face of God. Praise! Praise be upon You God for giving me a chance and making me feel like You always forgive me.

Forgive me, God.

<u>Savior?</u>

What an incredible question! Do I address myself directly to God? Do I ask Jesus into my life? I have FULLY accepted Jesus as my personal Savior, He is my only teacher. But do I pray to Him? He never tells me to in the Bible, even James says, "Draw nigh to God and God will draw nigh to you." It's always God in the name of Jesus Christ. I want to know what Savior means. I find myself asking and asking. Let it be with God now.

November 27, 1974

<u>Answers and Peaceful Comforts</u>

Oh! Tonight I feel with God so close and peaceful. Praise you Lord. Jesus art my Savior indeed. His teachings, His life, His spirit, His authority over evil is my saving grace. Come into my heart, my home, and my whole life and make me whole and perfect as my father in heaven is perfect. Praise be to His name. Thank you Lord and God.

Peace is with us now, and forever in the Lord.

The trials of discipleship are in front of us and I am needy and I am ready to face them in the knowledge and glory of my Master. My purpose to exemplify the Christ has begun in great joy and hope and love.

November 30, 1974

<u>Praising God</u>

Melody has mentioned that she is a bit apprehensive about the words, "Praise God," but our Master said, "Behold, I make all things new."

I too have felt a slight cringing from embarrassment because of the old "Jesus freaks" and their lip service and vain repetitions.

I would not use embarrassing words with someone they would embarrass. But praise God for the chance to know about 'em.

December 2, 1974

O God, look into my heart and see my desire to eternally emulate You—every day.

My job—to stay unspotted from the world, yet talk to the world in words it will understand—is such a demanding job.

Today has been such unconsciousness, I could hardly see with my new eyes. God! Please in Christ's name help me stay there. See my tears of desire to be with you. I have offended my wife and God by indulging in a debasing fight. Please forgive me. "Make right with your brother, before you pray to God"— 1st John.

I will go make it right now. Thank you.

Unconscious Testing

Well, now comes the real test. God has pulled me out of my pit of earthliness and set me firmly on the firm rock and has said, "Follow your master's teachings, keep My commandments, and give thanks to the highest holy one."

Now that Melody too hears the calling, we must travel together and keep ourselves clean inside as well as out, so that the Holy Ghost can dwell singularly in us and do through us God's holy work. Blessed be His name.

Thank you and praise you for this knowledge, Lord Jesus. My Savior and Master if you are listening I want to follow You, and I love You my Father's Son.

December 4, 1974

My Two Greatest Lessons Today

1. I am judging at such an uncontrollable rate that I fear I'm not making improvements in that area. So I must now be extra conscious before I enter every door or situation. To prethink "I will not judge, I will respect and see this person as a child of God in His image and likeness, reflecting His qualities of perfection."

2. Also I must every free opportunity give thanks to our Father for such incredible blessings He has given myself and

Melody and also the simple ones that make life itself possible and much more comfortable and promising. Praise and thank you Lord.

December 6, 1974
<u>A Bad Day</u>

I had a bad day yesterday. I didn't call on God at my work. My work showed of total nonconsciousness. I learned that I must first during and after every day's events pray to God, ask for help, and praise His name and His countless gifts and blessings to us, because without God, like yesterday, my life is dead.

That is why nothing was written in here yesterday, for I didn't feel worthy nor capable of writing in My New Life Book, for yesterday I truly was emulating my old, empty, purposeless life. Praise God, my Redeemer in my Savior's name, Christ Jesus.

December 31, 1974, Quebec, Canada, Room 612
<u>Looking Back and It Is Beautiful</u>

Hello, my old friend, My New Life Book. The reason I haven't written in 17 days is I have been living my old life, but tonight an angel came to me and I opened My New Life Book for the first time since December 14th, and read some previous pages and oh, the Spirit filled me with purpose and desire to live with the Lord, instead of the boredom, homesickness, and deviation-seekingness of the last few days.

Oh praise You and thank You Lord for opening my eyes that were swollen shut with the devil's subtle heat.

I aim to serve You now and forever, but especially now, always now makes forever.

1975

January 1, 1975, Hotel, Lobby Sofa, Quebec

It's 10:50 AM Wednesday, New Year's Morn. Well, here I am on the other side in a New Year. Very depressed, very unhappy. Before I felt so high, Christ was in our room perceivably and I had my delicate balance. But Satan, that devil, turned me around and rendered me so helpless, so un-in-control of myself. I have cried already this year. I haven't praised God.

Oh, God praise you! See me inside. I am fighting and it feels like I'm fighting alone. I need your arm to fight with/for me. Please, I'm yours. Come here, Jesus, right here and SAVE ME!!!

January 13, 1975

Heard reports of the second little earthquake in a 24-hour period here in southern California. It frightened me and I started getting super heavy earthquake vibes. I called Mel and told her if there was one to stay out and I'd even walk to her in Woodland Hills.

January 19, 1975

A lot of the unspiritual signs are reappearing and I pray for a renewal of help. One of the evenings we were reading our book together (Old Testament in novel form) and I was touched by Jacob consecrating his life to the Lord God and was compelled to do the same immediately. While doing so, I made a statement concerning "denying the works and life of the devil." And the word "deny" slipped from my mind like a stolen piece of fruit. I opened my thesaurus and looked up the word "abstain" and found a whole slew of put-downs for the devil and his whole trip. His many disguises and faces and forms. It was inspiring to say the least.

January 28, 1975

Stopped at the Little Brown Church where Mel and I got married and prayed intensely.

Yesterday while driving through Coldwater Canyon this very thought entered my mind, "Life is <u>so</u> intense!!"

February 8, 1975

<u>Called Again</u>

Out of the gloomy despair of a dope-clouded mind came the call to New Life, the Christian calling again.

After forsaking the Lord to escape from my conscience and my path (my own self-discipline), for the cloudy shroud of constant smoking and playing so self-assured at the Bla Bla Cafe—I felt the despair surround me and the Christian angel called me, saying "come to my fold."

O Lord, forgive me, forgive me, take me in again, again, please my dear Lord, in Christ Jesus' name. Praise God who never forgets, but always forgives. My perfect Father, I want to be with you—and perfect too.

February 23, 1975

<u>The Calling</u>

Oh, I feel the calling so strong tonight. To join the holy army and fight the numbness in the world toward God. Even the very belief in the existence of God is a battle. But when I truly believe in God and I have to fight the insidious evils around me—and more horrifying, right inside me—I find myself feeling beaten and hearing those Satanic words, "Give up, you're too human. Only the saints, priests, monks, and nuns are clean enough from the world and its forms to reach the Lord God and be chosen for holy service."

Please, God, in Christ's name and teachings, I want to be chosen to be with you in Armageddon. I want to forsake the evil one now!! On your side only! No possibilities of any other master or side or path or pseudo light, belief, or god.

I want to die for you God and be reborn a <u>whole</u> disciple. Living, emulating, and shining Your will, teachings, and bearing fruits everyday to everyone.

I love you God. And I know You love me!

The devil hates me more every day. He despises me more the closer I get to you. He's losing his grip. Praise You God. Your light is the only thing I want to see and the only thing I want to reflect. Blessed be Your will.

February 24, 1975

I feel a fountain spewing clear, clean spirit waters in my being. I feel a light glowing around me—but it's the Lord's light, not mine—and I feel a peace with God.

I believe now that Melody and I can make it. I can be chosen for the Army of the Lord to do battle with that evil devil, mortal mind, false belief, liar. And see the glory of the Father, Son, and Holy Spirit and be in New Jerusalem.

If only I give all the glory to God, I remain humble and give all the credit to God to keep the commandments and love my brothers and sisters. Praise God my Redeemer. Amen.

February 25, 1975

Bless the day I accepted Your Son, God, as my personal Savior. Jesus Christ is come in the flesh and the devil trembles as I write His name. Praise You God for Your wonderful Son, my Lord Jesus. Amen!

February 28, 1975

Sick and Sleeping

My purpose is to do your will and serve your plan, to spread the holy teachings of Jesus the Christ to the people through music. But my purpose is undermined daily by the subtle serpent, always trying to get me to write useless songs.

Here I am, heart opened like a book. Do you see evil intentions in my heart Lord? If you do, please burn them out with all expedience. I want to do your will so intensely. I know the answer is to daily pray to you and write to you and listen for you and read the holy writings. Praise to you my God.

I only want to please You with my life. Help.

March 12, 1975

Music Is Important

Sometimes I think of my role in this life and I get confused. Trying to decide "why am I here?" My life is so revolved around music that it sometimes makes me neglect my duty to consciously acknowledge God every day.

Reading in The Greatest Book Ever Written I was fascinated by the story of David's life. How much music played a part in his calling. The psalms and his commission to play for King Saul which led to so much.

Music is my medium in which to serve and praise God. I am compelled now to strive for an audience from the general music listening world, to get a platform in which to do the will of God by telling Jesus' stories, parables, and messages in a new refreshing way. After all, Jesus talked in parables to bring the common everyday person's understanding closer to God. And He did it in a way unsurpassed and more ageless than any story-teller in history. I feel my job is to retell His messages in their whole original meaning, in a contemporary way.

God has prepared me in my childhood with the interest, training, parents, and most blessed gift of all: the feeling I have in music as a fish feels in water.

Blessed be the day when God called me.

And blessed be every day I answer the calling and fulfill His holy will. Those days are few, but they're the only worthy ones and the only ones with any meaning or reason for being here.

March 13, 1975

Wow, this winter has been a teeter-totter, up and down, very Christian-called time. I guess I've felt consistently closer and more conscious of God and Jesus than any other period in my life. These times are the most uncertain times I've ever lived and they might be the most anyone's ever lived in, but that would be pretentious.

March 23, 1975
Feelings

I've been feeling called again to some of the Lord's music. To write more parable music. O God, it's such a fight. People don't believe in You. I do! I do! So much!

I've been writing commercial music to open the channels, get the platform, and retell the story of Jesus. His life, His miracles, His ministry, His salvations, and His finger always pointing upward to the Father who sent Him! Oh if I could only feel this way all the time. Lord God, I ask you in Jesus Christ's name, my Master unto You, let me feel like this all my waking hours, that my dreams and my sleeping hours be filled with Your visions, so that I may be a servant truly, totally unto You. And that I might be a lampstand on which to place Your light of truth and salvation.

WE ARE LOST without Your law. Please give me the gift of total discipleship. I may not be worthy yet, but my desire is fully ripe to serve You. Why must I struggle so? Why must I be tempted so?

It is written that "man shall serve the Lord as God and <u>only</u> Him shall he serve."

So let it be in our lives God. Please in Christ's name, I knock at the door for your glory. Father, please give me the gift of conscious Christian mind. You know my needs, Father, I love You and trust You with all my heart and soul. Now let me do so with my mind.

March 25, 1975

Spring arrives, my life reopens its eyes. Everything is new again. I pray to be completely reborn in Christ's name. To follow His example and to be His disciple in totalness. But mainly that rebirth! I am watching for a sign in my life. It will come soon, I pray. I feel. Thank you for Melody, music, my very life, and Your Son.

March 28, 1975

It's Starting

This morning I felt the beginnings of my prayers being answered. I felt drawn to think of Jesus.

Last November during my "high Christian week," I conquered worldly problems by thinking, "What would Jesus do?"

And I almost always found the right answer and an incredible sense of peace. Praise God.

So this morning a missing connection was reconnected and I have the powerful tool to use against problems and decisions. And Satan. Jesus was a perfect man, I pray to be likewise.

April 1, 1975

Dark Before the Dawn?

I've felt frustrated and a bit depressed the past few days. Everything I'm trying to do musically is futile. Spiritually I have not been high. It is discouraging.

I feel so helpless in my desire to have musical success. It all seems to be on human (success) levels that I desire it, but I know that there are spiritual reasons and spiritual ways and means to my life and purpose.

Lord God, I pray to be comforted through this wait. Give me strength in Christ Jesus' name. Help me be patient.

April 2, 1975

Wrote "Straight and Narrow" with Randy Stonehill. Over to Keith Carradine's and played backgammon. Wrote a song called "I'll Never Forget Your Face." Keith wrote the lyrics, and I wrote the music.

Melody and I had a big fight over her drinking coffee and we made an agreement that if she gave up drinking coffee I would give her two piano lessons a week and we would write together at least once a week. No use telling me that she kept her promise and I didn't. To this day I don't give her any lessons and we hardly write together at all on a regular basis. I really feel bad about this...Praise the Lord, we learn from the past.

April 24, 1975

<u>Randy Wimer My Brother</u>

Today Randy called me, we talked mostly about religion. Two things stood out as possible considerations. One, that the Sabbath day (that we both agree is Saturday) should be kept holy and no work should be done therein, from sundown Friday to sundown Saturday. Also that Christ may be our/the Creator of the world and us and all in it. Please help us to find out the answers, Father, in Christ's name.

April 25, 1975

<u>First Sabbath with Knowledge</u>

[Keith talks about breaking the Sabbath by eating with friends, and about worldliness.]

Please forgive me these possible trespasses in this time as I'm searching for the truthful answer, from You Lord about the Sabbath and how literally I must observe it. How important is it? Please let me know with as much detail as possible. Thank you Father, in Jesus' name.

April 27, 1975

Picked up Randy Wimer and went to Lancaster. Met his parents, ate Mexican food, heavy rap. Religious experiences discovering the Holy Ghost.

[Six months later, Keith added:]

This night in Lancaster, Randy and I were arguing about the validity of Scripture as totally accurate and inspired word for word. Randy kept claiming the Holy Spirit is the source of his translation and interpretation, and then something clicked inside and on the way home, tears filled my eyes and I was filled with the Holy Spirit, and from that day on nothing's been a struggle comparatively, concerning my walk with God.

May 6, 1975
The Holy Ghost

Last Monday I discovered the knowledge of the existence of the Holy Ghost. As the personal vehicle through which the Son comes into our lives.

And the Son is the same in respect to the Father.

I feel so strong, my love for the Father and my trust in the Father. I am learning to love the Son and only now seeing the need to acknowledge a third entity. Separate in identity, but one with the others in purpose. Please Father in Christ Jesus' name bring the Holy Ghost into my life, and baptize me. Amen.

May 9, 1975

MAJOR DAY!!!!! I went to the beach and the Getty Museum. Ate at the beach then Mel and I went to Randy Stonehill's and we all went to Beverly Hills to the Vineyard Christian Fellowship. *[Here Keith heard the pure gospel message and raised his hand high in the air to give his heart to Jesus.]*

Then I had to leave for my Goodbye Charlies gig. It was so sleazy I quit.

June 8, 1975

I played in church. This was the first time. This was Baptism day. Then we all went down to the beach and we got baptized along with a lot of others. It was so fantastic! Mel and I were baptized together. We were all so close, I'll never forget it.

June 15, 1975

We went to Kathryn Kuhlman's miracle service. It was truly impressive and inspiring. At the end I got real depressed and drained until I realized God didn't want me basing my faith on emotions.

June 16, 1975

It Happened!

Well, the Holy Spirit has entered our lives and we have a fellowship to go to. New faith and miracles!!

It's wonderful. I know the Father so much more personally through knowing Jesus so much more personally through knowing the Holy Spirit for the first time.

We love His holy name and He's bestowing us with so many new friends and so much new music, so many holy songs. Our purpose is becoming so much clearer. My ministry is coming into view.

New friends: Matthew, Kenn, Terry, Mary, Richard, and Paul.

Old friends who now know the Lord: Todd, Jay, Debbie, and Randy Wimer.

Old friends who've been touched or are near: Susie, Connie, Mel's Aunt Gerdie, and Mel's mother.

Bless you Jesus cause you've blessed the Father by saving us all through Your bloody death. Amen.

June 19, 1975

Bought Bibles and crosses at the Gospel Bookstore in Canoga Park. Picked up a hitchhiker and bought him lunch and took him to Terry's until he said he'd like to pray with us. Then off to the Bla. First Thursday night. I got fired from Saturday because of attendance. $67.00. Then we had another all night meeting till dawn. We cast out demons until we found the secret. Jesus' name. We knew this before but we learned it through experience. We actually heard Satan leave. Great night.

June 24, 1975

Went to Marlene and Leonard's for dinner, backgammon, and heavy-duty witness. We left on not too good terms. The Lord was teaching us what sensitive witness was.

June 25, 1975

Me, Mel, and Todd wrote "You've Got It Comin' To You."

July 4, 1975, Dallas

<u>Now</u>

Wow, the Holy Spirit has cleaned up my life so much. I'm on my way to New York to save my Grandmother. I should say to give her the Lord, the good news about her Savior. Thank You Father for revealing Your Son....Words are worthless to express the magnitude of gratitude I feel. Oh thank you.

July 8, 1975, 3:00 AM, New York

<u>I miss Melody!</u>

July 27, 1975, 3:00 AM

<u>Not a Fanatic</u>

Please Lord, keep me sensitive to the spiritual needs of those who need Your Salvation. Please keep making me wise as a serpent and harmless as a dove, Lord. Praise You.

People can get wary of my company if I go off the deep end and only witness from my plane instead of going to where they are and showing them I care for them individually.

Lord change me, get rid of any radical tendencies. Help me control my "overwhelming enthusiasm." Make me unselfish, unproud, quiet and full of humility and gentleness.

Father I love You. You showed me Your gift to me, Jesus.

October 16, 1975
Still with Jesus

Oh praise the Lord. I'm still with Jesus. He's changed my life so completely. I'll be 22 on Tuesday.

Fellowship is so fantastic. The end is almost here. The Holy Spirit is gathering crops for the Lord's harvest and He will re-appear in shining glory. Jeweled and crowned. Oh He deserves our praise. I can't wait until I see Him coming. O Lord we're here waiting for Your return.

December 14, 1975
Oppression

I am in a time of oppression from the enemy, stemming from my many faults and people I have stepped on coming back and wanting repentance—which is necessary, but my pride is great.

The enemy is attacking on all fronts. Guilt, helplessness about personality-related faults, and condemnation are burying me. I am surrounded with problems. Also not doing, reading, and praying enough. Lord, save me from Satan and myself in Jesus' name.

December 22, 1975
More Progress

Last night after watching an old touching Christmas movie the Lord touched me and led us into prayer. He said to me in essence, "Ask anything now, abiding in Me, and you will receive it, anything." So I asked for all the desires of my heart, total riddance of my faults, my parents' salvation, and prayed for special unsaved or fallen people. I feel more assurance today than ever before.

Give me wisdom O Lord to know who will be saved, who is a counterfeit, and who is just empty and fillable.

1976

March 14, 1976

Sunday church, then counseled with Kenn and Tony about our problems. The answer was simple, whenever you're having problems with someone, thank God for that person in your life, just the way he is. Don't ask for God to change him until he is through using him in your life. Praise God. Went to Gabriel Ferrer's to play tennis. Then to Chino Youth Jail. People got saved.

March 23, 1976

<u>Trials and Tickled</u>

What a magical Lord we have. He spins our trials into gold. He turns every curse into a blessing for His true children. He is a wonderful God.

Randy Stonehill and I are bosom buddies at last, it's such a miracle only because it's not just between us, it's him and it happened all at once. The ice broke and now he finally sees the new me. Hallelujah.

If the Lord allows Satan to hand us a trial and we squirm, it grows into something more ugly. But if we embrace the trial and claim the victory on faith and praise God for it, then it ceases to be a trial. We really welcome and enjoy it as a wonderful chisel that is making a flawlessly cut jewel for our Lord's glory.

Cut on, my Lord, my King, my Maker.

March 23, 1976

Claim It

We Christians accept nothing compared to the bountiful faith the Lord expects us to have. We accept sickness, arguments, and mountains in our way, instead of casting them into the sea with one word in our Lord's name. We're all cowards. And afraid to step out on the water. Put our_selves_ on the line. But we should never tempt God. The secret is learning the difference between tempting him and calling on him to answer, or stepping out in faith.

Teach me all three of these lessons Lord, bring them into my heart. Make me: one, a prayer warrior, two, a trial embracer, and three, a mountain mover in Jesus.

March 27, 1976, Saturday

Flew to Sacramento. First concert was a bit in the flesh. Was anxious about how many people came and how much I would receive. Sin. Then the second was as good as the first wasn't good. The Spirit anointed me and I felt wonderful. Praise God.

April 9, 1976, New York

[Keith was flown to New York to audition for one of the most powerful men in secular recording. Keith still wanted to bring Jesus to the world using song parables.]

Did a Bible study, went for Japanese food. Went to CBS, then went for my appointment with Clive Davis. He kept us waiting for almost two hours. It was a failure, but I took it so well I couldn't believe it…kept telling myself that the Lord wanted me to do a Christian album. It depressed me, but I kept my chin up.

April 10, 1976, New York

Called Buck Herring and told him I thought the Lord wanted me to do a Christian album. He bore witness.

Called the cab after ordering a genuine Pizza Stop pizza for Mel. At the airport I discovered some Krishna people and a bunch came on the flight. It bothered me so much that I decided to write one of them a note which read, "Only Jesus is Lord of All." Then the Lord gave me a melody, and I will have a song soon. Went home and had pizza and brownies.

April 11, 1976

Got up and went to church. It bored me and distressed me.

September 28, 1976

Where Things Are Clear

We are nothing but dust. Our lives are not ours. Our bodies are not ours. Our future is in Your hands.

The Lord is making me ready to die—completely—I don't deserve to live—so come Spirit of Holy God—live instead of me.

There is no joy left in life but to realize I am nothing and let God be what He is—all.

Tears cannot express nor laughter His grace/gifts. I am His.

Please Keith! Don't ever go back—look up—it's time to go.

December 30, 1976

Busted

I've been laid low by my mouth. I've been attacked by my own tongue. I dug a pit and fell in.

1977

April 20, 1977
<u>Why?</u>

Lord, why are Your children so blind? They don't love one another—and my own flesh is warring against You and Your commandments.

Lord save us.

I see almost all Christians falling away from Your words. Getting fat off Your grace, but not doing Your will.

Lord, my brothers and sisters are losing ground as the devil takes over and power is given to him to prevail and overcome the saints. Lord Jesus come quickly.

Help, we are lost and falling and need You. I repent of unrighteous judgment but I don't want to be blind too—tell me what to do and how to die. Help.

September 18, 1977
<u>Milk and Meat</u>

It's time for revival in my heart of hearts. I've learned that milk is truth that's been digested by someone else, like a teacher, then they feed it to you. Meat comes only directly from God and has to be sought like manna—gathered.

I am so rotten and lately I've been walking so in the flesh. Blind because of three things. My full, full schedule, my pride, and the enemy.

Please Father, continually remind me of how Your patience is running out with time, and give me the ability to have the Spirit walk. Make all things new. I'm somewhat jaded. Give me a new view from You. Bless and praise to God and Son and Spirit.

1978

January 6, 1978

Help!! Help!!

I'm being squeezed out. Nothing left but me and the Spirit. Me, oh I hate the old me. Why do I continue to be so used by God if I am so selfish and carnal and me????

I've been feeling satisfied with my walk lately, and I feel that that must be a sin, "thinking you are something, when you are nothing." But the Spirit holy is real.

I'm so sick of all this, so desperately in need of a voice from above. Heck, I've heard the voice, it tells me to pray, to go away and fast and pray, to pray for hours every day, but I can't do that!! I'm so lazy and busy and "spiritual" already. Please God make me a prayer warrior, a warrior against sin and flesh and the devil and the world, against me, the old rotten me.

January 7, 1978

I'm Only Human, He's Only God

I'm only human—He's only God
I'm only selfish—He's only love
I'm only proud—He's only God
I'm only dying—He's only life
I'm only stupid—He's only wisdom
I'm only nothing—He's only all
Help!

January 21, 1978

Mel drove me to LAX and I sat next to Fred, a black brother whom the Lord has called. I witnessed to him. He said he'd been to the cross and turned back. He said he'd come to my concert, but didn't show at the luggage place. Got ripped off by big "D"!

Concert was not anything special except I got new things—went to a brother's to sleep. Ate and read. Many saved and lordified.

January 22, 1978, Kansas City

Up. "Token prayer." 11:00 AM service, worship. I was grieved because praise took the place of repentance and consecration.

The Lord taught me that revival comes from three things, one repentance, two prayer, three unity. All together, alone, at the same time—or consecutive, but they <u>must</u> happen, all of them or we're sunk—dying, dead, and buried.

Oh God, help with the Vineyard, help with Kenn, help with me. Show me the way...I love You God. Help.

Concert. I shared tonight and I read the Word and preached. Many were broken, but there's still so much of me in my ministry, and I need a total breaking and cleaning out. I know there are major crises coming....I only pray You let me keep my wife Melody, for I need her love and help although Your grace is sufficient unto me. Please spare her to stay with me, I will give You far more love than her, and all my love for her is for You Jesus.

Take anything, but leave my Melody. Please God, but I am willing to suffer all loss if it is Your precious will. I am Yours.

Home in the morning. Bye Bye Lord. Your baby.

February 12, 1978, 4:00 AM, Orlando, Florida, Holiday Inn, Room 218

I'm so confused. I need repentance so badly. My spirit cries out within me to repent for I have sinned by judging and condemning and being bitter against the truth. By not praying for those the Lord has shown me are wrong.

Please teach me to have a clear conscience. Humble me Lord, break me please. Melody is Yours. "My" ministry is Yours. My body is Yours. Put me through Your fire, I want to fear You God. Please give me wisdom and teach me how to repent. Psalm 139, especially verses 21-24.

March 3, 1978

Today the Lord warned me not to entertain, welcome, or let "doubts" remain. I used to teach that Satan would play ping-pong and I was the net. He'd say, "You don't believe," and then say in the other ear, "Look at what a rotten Christian you are, thinking thoughts like that." I have been falling for that. Help Lord. Also, I've often said that I only grow in trials and whenever good times come I only grow complacent and start feeling like "I'm doing pretty good." And instead of seeing how much farther I have to go and praying for help and praising for what He's done, I lay back and stagnate.

I've gotta start growing in the good times, or bad times will be the only ones I know. Gotta go to second base this time.

May 1, 1978, May Day

Jesus gave me a new song today about the devil, called "Lies" and I'm excited because it may be the missing link for the album as yet untitled. Please Jesus give me a title.

My walk with Jesus has been poor lately due to my being too busy to pray or read, which means I'm too busy for Jesus and that's a sin. But I don't feel sinful. Just weak and frustrated.

Help Lord, please go ahead and spank me. I've never needed a spanking like now. I've lost my first love, maybe even my second love. And I'm becoming such a good ole Christian. I'm so sick of the whole trip.

I fear You God and I fear getting cold. Help please. This is a letter to You Lord and I know You answer Your mail a lot faster and better than I do. Again, help.

Signed Your guilty, disobedient son, Keith.

Fall 1978

I'm so afraid of power. Not God's power…my fleshly desire to rule others. In my heart of hearts, I only want to serve. To present the babes as mature men and women of God! I want more than anything else to pour myself out for them, for Jesus. But then there's my old nature that wants to control everything.

Lord I repent of my old nature and I give my fear of power to you. For you are the only true power, Jesus!! Control my life with your Spirit. Control the sheeps' lives with your Spirit—and if you use me, let me give thanks to you!! For you're the only true God and Savior!! Hallelujah! Let me continue to grow less important to me. I am so blind. Help me see.

1979

January 15, 1979

<u>Lord Help Again</u>

My Jesus, please pour Your strong life out on me, because I've grown so hard and cold and "spiritual." I'm almost dead. I need and desire to be close to you. I want it! So bad! Just to please You. Do you want me to move? Do you want me to quit doing the Newsletter? Is it all a fleshly soul trip? I need to know Your heart Lord, I don't want to be a Pharisee. Please God, You know I'm serious about this. Send Your angel to answer.

March 10, 1979

Our concert at Oral Roberts University [ORU] is cancelled. We're going anyway. In my spirit, I know it's right, but the rest of me is scared!

Had the best prayer/cry in a month. Oh! Did I cry!

March 11, 1979

In an hour and fifteen minutes the Vineyard will lay hands on us to go to Tulsa and I'm not totally sure we're supposed to go! Oh, my pride, reputation, and false faith all say, "Go." My mind and heart are divided. I can't find my spirit!...I must go for the right motives. God said, "Go!"

March 19, 1979, at ORU, 3 AM

Can't sleep. An angel wants to burn my lips with the coal. I must count the cost. Isaiah 6:7,8—"Here I am. Send me!"

I want to be God's voice, full of love, mercy, and fire! But I must be dead!

Prayer is the key. Make me a man of prayer!

God give me power/grace. I have zeal/fire and love/balance. Give me power/grace.

Put power in my words. Your Word is powerful! Make Your Word my word—make Your power my power.

I am ready for death!

Kill me, destroy me, burn me beyond recognition—I know now that You would never hurt or harm me. You only want me dead! Let it be done!

March 20, 1979, 12:00 PM

I don't want greatness. I want You to be great!

Lower me down, humble me. Teach me to humble myself, O Lord! I love You so much—but not as You love the Father. I want to love You that way!

March 22, 1979

Tuesday night was a strain. Yesterday all the elders from the Agape Force came and completely refreshed my spirit! Good prayer meeting last night.

O God, I was frightened, but now I'm feeling better that this is God's revival. His will, His burden, not mine.

Lord let me pray! Help me prepare a message in the furnace with You! "Not by power, not by might, but by My Spirit!"

Amen.

6:15 PM, dressing room, Maybee Center, ORU

Here goes—burn me now God—send a Pentecost!!!

March 24, 1979, 6:00 PM, dressing room, ORU

I'm so tired. My flesh is rebelling so hard. It doesn't want to have a prayer life. Help me O God.

Tonight I either live gloriously or die shamefully.

O Lord, I'm so lazy. I don't see how I can handle this kind of life for very long! Help!

[*A few weeks after returning from ORU, Keith took a long weekend away to fast and pray for direction.*]

April 17, 1979, 1:30 AM, Room 201, Royal Knight Hotel, Big Bear Lake, CA

Help. I flattered myself with the whole armor of God knight stuff and got a sleazy room.

Running scared, lost the whole vision, the whole fire—still dying. Gasping for air! Help, God/Jesus. I'm sick, I'm drowning, and I'm taking my family and ministry down with me…I'm so brave until the war starts with my flesh, "I buffet my body and make it my slave, lest possibly after preaching to others, I myself may become disqualified." Help me buffet my body.

April 17, 1979, 5:00 PM

Here I am, waiting. Scared, bored, hungry. Unbelieving, frustrated, even mad at God for making me go through this.

I preach against easy grace and then when it isn't easy, I get mad at God for making it just the way I preach it!!! Oh! The total hypocrisy of it all!!

Please forgive me. Daddy, break me, and for Your sake, speak to me now please!!

I've never been a follower. I've been a leader all my life, but now I want to follow You.

April 17, 1979, 8:40 PM, cabin

I have begun to feel the Holy Spirit's presence. I have such a long way to go.

I have no idea what it must be like to live without talents, possibilities, chances for greatness. It is a curse, I know. But I must employ them for they are gifts of God.

O God, what great blessing You could have through my life if I were…a clean, sanctified vessel.

This blessing for you, this glorification of Your throne and name—I want. But if You would get more joy from me doing other things, from being obscure, like Rees Howells…

What do You want of me??

10:00 PM

I cried a great cry at the hopelessness of it all! Good break, but now what?

Your pleasure is all I seek, nothing else matters. Thank you for showing me that.

I still am embarrassed when You tell me to witness.

April 18, 1979, 11:05 AM

Awoke at 9:30. Been reading <u>The Hidden Life of Prayer</u> that Leonard Ravenhill gave me...

April 18, 1979

Josiah's birthday, 7 months.

[It was at this time that Keith, so very grateful to God for his family, became convinced that God was calling him to commit everything to His keeping, including his family. The result was the song "Pledge My Head to Heaven."]

Well, I pledge my head to heaven for the gospel.
And I ask no man on earth to fill my needs.
Like a sparrow up above,
I am enveloped in his love.
And I trust him like those little ones he feeds.

Well, I pledge my wife to heaven for the gospel.
Though our love each passing day just seems to grow...
As I told her when we wed,
I'd surely rather be found dead,
Than to love her more than the one
Who saved my soul

I'm your child,
And I wanna be in your family forever!
I'm your child, and I'm gonna follow you
No matter, whatever the cost,
Well I'm gonna count all things loss.

Well, I pledge my son to heaven for the gospel,
Though he's kicked and beaten,
Ridiculed and scorned.
I will teach him to rejoice
And lift a thankful, praising voice.
And to be like him who bore the nails
And crown of thorns.

Well, I've had my chance to gain the world
And to live just like a king,
But without your love
It doesn't mean a thing!

Well, I pledge my son…I pledge my wife…
I pledge my head to heaven.
I pledge my son…I pledge my wife…
I pledge my head to heaven for the gospel.

April 18, 1979, 4:50 PM, cabin

I believe God said I'll be clear by 9 PM to go home, sleep, possibly break fast in the morning. I'm reading Philippians 1:21-26, doubted Paul's sincerity here. God said, "Who are you to doubt My Word?" If it's in the Bible, then it's sincere! Praise God for faith.

I have a bitter, rebellious spirit against God. It's been coming out in my prayers. A real snotty, bad attitude. Not my usual love and trust, unless that's all phony and God is revealing what my heart is saying to him all the time—yech, how does He put up with it?

Kill me God, there is no good in me, I am wretched through and through. I have served Your enemy before and even since the revival. My whole nature needs to change. I am helpless, more than since I first got saved. Even more so, because I have no Christian hope in myself! I am smelling foods that aren't there—my body is flipping out on this fast. My muscles and stomach ache. I am doing it to maneuver God! Not for His glory. Help, help please.

I write. I can't pray. I scream inside, but not enough to cry. When I cry I get so excited I'm finally crying that I quit crying. Help! I'll try and pray again. Glory to Jesus...

Angels are here with me. The room is full...

April 22, 1979

It's been good making myself read the ten chapters and having family worship with the girls and Mel. It's been a good example and I'm not listening to my flesh which says, "Oh, you're becoming legal! God won't honor this forced prayer stuff!" Well, there are times when the Spirit's grieved by my "clockwatching" soul, but there are good times of prayer and I believe they will form into godly habits. Not to mention the blessing that comes from obedience and a clear conscience being a good witness to my wife and children and building a new foundation for the future. How to maintain this on the road will be the big question.

Lord, please help Your servant be consistent and put You first, always!

Lack of prayer is sin.

Legal prayer is sad.

<u>Freedom</u> is best.

May 2, 1979

Tony Salerno came and ministered to me about meditation of the Word. Praise God. My vows were too hard. They were made in sin. Please Jesus let me out of them, "legally," and let me develop into a man of God through Your discipline. My intentions in this "vow" were to get to know You and I want to do that any way I can.

Please lead me into an hour of prayer a day without me timing it. God doesn't want me serving Him under obligation but out of love. Praise You Jesus.

May 3, 1979, 5:00 PM

Had an incredible time with the Lord in His Word yesterday. Learned about the Resurrection power of Jesus through suffering—rejoicing.

May 13, 1979, 4:00 AM

I _love_ the Newsletter, printing, folding, the community—I have _very little_ affection for the Word and prayer.

Please give me that love for Your Word and prayer or free me from the bondage of this predicament—holy calling. I want so to obey you, to be disciplined, but you've got to help me. Do something, Lord. It's my fault, but Your move. I'm stagnating watching the ship go down, helplessly standing by, limp and powerless, I'm defeated. Help me. Numb and tearless, waiting for a word, a miracle, please free me Jesus.

It's all fading, just memories, nothing current. Sure! Concerts, records, ministry, but worthless trash compared to the potential. O God, do something. I'm here begging you, please give me a vision, "with no vision, the people perish, are unrestrained." I've got to see Your will for me, the people here are looking for leadership and I'm floundering. It's no better than a month ago. Oh what can I do? I'm desperate, yet nonchalant. I'm in a hypnotic state, "oh everything will work out." The things are in Jesus' hands and people are continuing to grow. I'm getting to the end of my long rope. Corner me Lord!

May 15, 1979, 5:00 PM

On Sunday I felt the Lord say that the cloud was gonna lift soon. Praise God.

June 2, 1979, Hawaii Concerts

Jimmy and Carol Owens' guest house. The cloud is lifting! I have been under the <u>law</u>, "severed from Christ, fallen from grace," Galatians 5.

Because I've been under my own preaching—"seeking to be justified by the works of the flesh," vows, promises, <u>self-improvements</u>, and discipline. God's proved it to me. I'm incapable. I can't <u>do</u> it. I've got to abide and let Him do it. There is a balance in this. Prayer, faith equals works, fruits.

June 3, 1979

Been home a half an hour. Feeling a little dazed. Hope to come into a new era. Praise You Jesus. After making out my will Jimmy Owens took me flying in Hawaii. Heavy. Jesus has great things in store, "but only what's done for Christ will last."

Give me eternal eyes. Let me see things in the light of eternity. Thank you for the faithful family at home. Please help with all the changes.

July 2, 1979, 4:40 PM

For the first time in months, I awoke with peace—<u>real peace</u>...

I can seek the Lord now, for an angel from God has come to minister to me. I love God so much, my heart overflows with quiet, gentle joy. My eyes water with tears for the peace in my soul. My faith is refreshed. My desire to commune with God and intercede for souls is renewed with power! My thirst for God's Word has greatly increased. The prison doors have swung open of themselves. The shackles have fallen to the ground. My heart is bursting with joy and <u>hope!</u> Oh! <u>I can hope again.</u>

Jesus I'm so grateful that there was no formula—no secret way to regain my peace. No amount of Bible reading or <u>forced</u> prayer time (on my part), brought this state on. But You, an answer to the desperate crying out of my heart, came and rescued me from the bondage of works and self-spirituality. I want to glory in Your presence. You want me to share Your glory, but only as a gift, not as a result of <u>my</u> efforts, but as a result of Your goodness, mercy, and love for me. Thank You for helping me hang on!

I love You Jesus, Father I can't thank You enough.

Spirit, guide me into the depth of Your grace.

July 3, 1979

The oppression is gone, the bad habits and residue remains. Gotta clean up from the storm. Help me Jesus please.

July 5, 1979, 2:00 AM

Pressure still gone, bad habits still remain.

The same God who removed the pressure can change me—I am willing to do anything. But unable to do much in the way of self-improvement—God, please clear the way for me to glorify You in my deeds. Please make me more like You for the first time in a long while. I not only believe You can change me, but I believe it's the only way you'll allow me to change—if You do it!

July 9, 1979

Harvey House. Concert for World Vision went well. Nine to ten thousand people. Went too long.

August 3, 1979, Noon

We're moving in about a month to Texas! My walk is about the same—I'm still fat, lazy, off schedule, and disobedient. Please help me Jesus. My heart's desire is increasing daily to be released from this prison. I'm ready. Help—help.

August 11, 1979, Sunday

<u>Grace</u> not works! Only <u>Jesus</u> saved me the first time, and only <u>Jesus</u> can save me now. I believe He is beginning a great redemption.

August 17, 1979

The Lord is showing me a lot about sovereignty. How we need <u>Him</u>, not we need to be more this or that. One quality matters, that we seek God. Thank You Lord for not letting me get deceived into thinking we could do it, that we could find some special secret and find revival fires—only <u>You</u> have the secret and it's You! Keep this before my eyes.

October 3, 1979, 3:00 AM, Texas Ranch

Just read the last six months of this journal and it's disgusting. The same thing over and over again. God gives me light and I respond and then fall, groveling in the dust, begging God for help. It's pitiful.

I'm almost blaming Him for not giving me that "grace" I so desperately need, but every time He visits me with His presence, I immediately blow it with the flesh. Disobeying or spiritual pride. I'm sick of being a worm for the devil and my domineering body. I know I need Your help, but I've got to do what You command.

To ask You to help me is to repeat myself for the 1,000th time. I do ask You to help me, but I've got to pick myself up and seek Your face!

My mom came for a visit this last weekend and it was good. I'm praying about whether to join Agape Force Ministries or make an album in L.A. Please direct.

We leave for the road tomorrow. I'm really excited. Jesus we need You for revival. Let us not seek anyone or anything else.

There's so much opportunity for self-righteousness, and to get a "martyr complex" about not charging for records or concerts. Also the mailing list is about to double with the next tour, which means more temptation with money, time-wasting, pride about Newsletter, etc.

The Lord has been opening doors to foreign ministry next year. Praise Him. I'm ready to go in my soul. Money is less important.

November 29, 1979

[Keith is in Honolulu on his way to Australia.]

The ministry is on an even keel. God is looking out for us. Getting close to Leonard Ravenhill.

Been writing songs with Mel for the new album. I love you Jesus. Help me rest.

Walking in the Spirit is like walking on a tightrope. It's a lot easier to walk on the ground—down to earth—than in the heavenlies. You can fall so easily. I still haven't learned how to get back on the rope when I fall. I have to wait until I either accidentally stumble on the tightrope or God literally lifts me up out of my stupor and puts me on it again.

I thank You Jesus for giving me this time alone with You, away from my ministry, community, even my beloved wife and children. I'm so grateful to get away and take a good, long objective look at it all.

Lord, I have the potential to move the world if I'll but die to myself, my ministry, even my potential.

Thank You for the prayers of the saints at home and all over. I know it's their faithfulness and Yours, not mine, that is bringing this awakening to start.

Living by faith is always "living without scheming."

December 12, 1979, 3:30 AM, Adelaide, Australia

In a quick and powerful answer to prayer, God, using Winkie Pratney, pinpointed the base of my frustrations, condemnations, failure, and miseries—lack of personal discipline. I see that lack of self-discipline is keeping my holiness (which I already have in Jesus) from controlling my life and coming to the surface. This is a brand-new view, and I believe I have isolated the enemy's greatest stronghold at this time in my life.

Winkie said, "There's nothing wrong with your spiritual life, Keith—it's the physical bad habits of a spoiled childhood. Sleeping late, slothfulness, laziness, not making a bed, doing dishes, or showering, eating too much, etc., etc. Those are the things that are making you frustrated, confused, and open to attack and condemnation."

Satan has been attaching lots of "spiritual lies" to my physical bad trip. And I've caught him. Now it's time to start working on changing those habits. Thank You Jesus. Help Lord. Now we know where to begin.

I now realize what I have to do to be happy in Jesus, or I should say, how to express the joy I already have in my heart in Jesus. Winkie says, "Take it in faith-size bites."

Freedom without bounds is mayhem, confusion, anarchy, and dangerous!

December 17, 1979, 1:40 AM, Australia

Got up with grumbly attitude about church service this morning. Service went well, I preached and refused to sing (I hope it wasn't all in the flesh that I refused to sing, Lord show me). Had a tremendous problem with my attitudes towards tonight's church service. It was a "X"-mas pageant and I found myself having to be in it!!!!! I still can't believe I did it. I might have been wrong to participate, but my grumbly attitude was definitely out of place. Concert went real well.

I see one of the enemy's greatest tricks was to attach personal physical discipline to devotional discipline. I would try to read 10 chapters and pray an hour a day, a very spiritual and noble desire to accomplish, but quite a hill to tackle all at once—when I'd fail, I'd drop everything I was trying to accomplish. "Faith-size bites"—that's the key!

December 18, 1979, 12:04 AM, Sydney

Discipline is not holiness—nor the way to holiness—it just helps you maintain it.

December 19, 1979, 1:45 AM, Rockhampton

Looks like I have a real problem with nicely stating either opinion or truth—gotta work on it. Help me Jesus please. Forgive me this stuff.

December 20, 1979, 2:45 AM

I am perplexed and wondering whether or not God would have us ever mention money in return for products (tracks, tapes, records, etc.).

The Newsletter is not a product. The tracks, tapes, and records are somewhat, but we'll never turn away anyone who has no money, and we're not keeping nonbelievers from getting ministered to. And we're not making an industry out of it. Please guide us Father.

December 20, 1979, 3:40 PM

The Growth Syndrome

It's a mistaken idea that success means increasing numbers, finances, and popularity. I have had visions of great dormitories full of students and people getting rehabilitated. Great presses and computers—great numbers of office and printing staff—counselors, teachers, administrators.

O Father, how I praise you for killing this soulish natural pipe dream. For commanding us to quit seeking growth and only seek You. Thank You for saving us from grave and foolish mistakes. No more people unless You obviously guide.

The only two areas I want to grow in are (1) true personal holiness and (2) effectiveness from heaven's point of view in our ministry.

December 24, 1979, 2:15 AM, Home

Arrived in Dallas at 1:40 AM last night. Mel is 8 months pregnant but she picked me up at DFW and I drove home. Got up early to play with my boy, Josiah. What a blessing!

December 29, 1979

Mel is gonna have the baby two weeks early.

1980

February 7, 1980, 6:45 AM, Recording in L.A.

Bethany Grace. My new daughter has been keeping me awake. She was born at 10:19 AM, February 5, two days ago, to God's glory.

I've just been reading the end of my lost, now found, spring diary where Mel and I fell in love, and I really started praying to Jesus. I was selfish, confused, helplessly fleshy—my relationships with my loved ones were selfish and touchy.

As I look at myself now I see the "same ole man," more patient, compassionate, mature, and wise—yes, but still so soulish and disappointing to Jesus. No real discipleship.

Inside of me is trapped a loving, sincere disciple of Jesus—regenerated, Spirit filled, saved by grace, but trapped by my lack of mature, strong choices and a host of ungodly habits.

[Recording] sessions have been going great. The Newsletter's about the only thing that really satisfies my thirst for growing, creative fulfillment. Even music seems too easy.

I'm such a spoiled child who needs excitement all the time.

I'm not really any better than before in my life, except I have more "knowledge," which unhappily makes me <u>even</u> more a wretch.

If I or anyone else ever reads this journal, it will probably seem real depressing and redundant. How long will God put up with me?? 70 times 7, and more?

February 8, 1980

Lord, I pray with everything in my heart, please give me a permanent change!! I want not only to be Your representative and ambassador to the people in the world and church publicly, but more importantly I want to be a constant, unchanging vessel of Your mercy, peace, and joy here and now, to my family, friends, and all who know me and have to live and work with me. That is my greatest desire, to be like You. Please grant Your servant this petition, which I am <u>certain</u> is Your expressed will for my life! (1 John 5:14,15).

February 9, 1980

The Lord is leading my heart into the knowledge that I REALLY CAN'T DO IT!!

He won't let me do it. His glory is magnified by His Holy Spirit doing the whole work. Just like at Pentecost! The only "work" that I <u>must</u> do is "abide and believe." Only by trusting Him and resting in Him can I do anything! It is my only hope of peace, or joy, or attainment of Christlikeness.

Met an old school acquaintance and didn't even try to witness to her. I guess I'm "officially lukewarm" and need to return to my first love! What a drag.

February 11, 1980

O Lord, my God, fill up my thirst with love for Yourself. God I need you right now. Be my lover, and my brother, and friend.

March 1, 1980, still in L.A.

There's a whole new consciousness of God's patience, love, and grace. How He loves me! That's such an incredible revelation to me, I want to sing out in joy. The album's going great.

Last night Bob Dylan came over to Buck's and we all played our albums. The fellowship was so sweet. Bob might be playing harmonica on my album. Gotta get my motives completely right.

June 3, 1980
<u>So Long!</u>

It's been quite a while since the last few sparse entries. A revival in February '79 changed my whole life with some sweeping, lasting changes. We went to Tulsa in March '79 to change the whole world (but only changed some lives—oh well!). Praise the God of my soul!

Then came the hardest year of my life. The "darkness of God" set in and the tortures of the law and my own nature struggled with each other. Oh what a fight. Some relief came a few months ago when the Lord started me on a slow but sure maturing program. After He proved to me there was no such thing as instant complete holiness (after all no one becomes mature spiritually or physically overnight). It's a much more regulated slow struggle, rather than trying to lose all your excess weight on a crash diet—one pound a week.

June 8, 1980

Hi. This book was lost over 7 weeks. Mel just found it again.

The last 2 months have been very good. The album got finished and they all got mailed out. I've been up all night for about 2 weeks working on the next Newsletter. Heaviest one yet. My heart has been through one of the best times in a long while.

The kids are so beautiful. I just don't deserve any of this.

Been spending lots of time with Leonard and Martha Ravenhill. They're just wonderful saints!

September 21, 1980, Sunday
<u>Gotta Keep Going</u>

Today, Leonard Ravenhill preached at church and boiled my blood and fired my soul so that my sins came up before me. God has been helping me lose my extra weight, both physically and spiritually. Very slowly. But I've been at a virtual standstill for about 6 weeks now.

Today the Lord showed me that I had gotten some new light lately, some new further grace, and that I had not tried to get rid of some faults and habits that before now have seemed impossible to overcome. He seemed to be saying that I had entered a new era of power and maturity. And that I could with this holy help start disciplining myself now with new strength, faith, and success, whereas before I was too in bondage to my flesh. I had received some deliverance in the past 6 months and was enabled to continue conquering my flesh and soul.

This is good news. A call to battle and arms. I know the fight will be brutally gruesome, but I also know it is <u>Him</u> who is calling me.

I have also been striving to have people move in the ministry. Recruiting—but the Lord has said that He wouldn't forsake us. Thank You Jesus.

November 10, 1980

Dear God,

I am failing again. I am busily doing nothing! I am not developing my relationship with you, with Melody, or with my kids. I am fastly spinning my wheels.

The Newsletter does not have priority. It is not getting done. The winter tour is not done. A lot of busy wastefulness is being accomplished—computers, office stuff, farm, cattle, horse stuff. I am losing ground and time.

Please Lord God, help me redeem the time.

I am so sorry. Tell me what is wrong with me. What can I do? Please help me with all this! Your black sheep—wanting to be white!

Keith

1981

March 29, 1981

I'm sincerely perplexed. My walk is at a standstill—though I'm gaining a few inches of ground, I still am fighting most of the same old battles. I am tired, weary of my lot as a minister and etc....I feel I have such potential to be of use to God, but alas, I am so useless right now.

I want to stop being popular with people and be popular with God.

Please don't give up on me Lord, please don't give up on me. Keep striving with me, Holy Spirit. I love You.

April 2, 1981, 3:26 AM, Sitting in my old garage sale recliner

The last entry made on different paper than the rest of this book, because this book had not been around or written in almost 10 months. As I read through this and the preceding yellow, "post-revival" book, which was found tonight after being lost for well over a year, I am not only disgusted but shocked that I could have changed or grown so little in 2 whole years.

Such sniveling! Such whining! I have been a basket case before God and I truly am ashamed of myself.

I'm in such a state of disgust with myself that I can only say that by God I am going to change. This cannot go on! I refuse it! God has given me a choice and He's made me able! Now let's go.

April 3, 1981, 3:52 AM

I can see by looking over my old writings that I have made a major philosophical mistake.

1. I have mistaken <u>desire</u> to do good with <u>doing</u> good, or at least being "counted as good by God."

2. I have mistaken the hatred and desire to give up sin, bad habits, hypocrisy, etc. with actually "giving them up"! I have deceived myself into believing that good intentions were going to bring about a natural reformation. That if I just had a pure heart with pure desires, that revival, renewal, and victory over sin were just around the corner!

Now I see that although "resolutions" themselves cannot actually bring about any lasting change—I can resolve with His grace and help to change, and then keep going—keep going—and blame no one but myself for failure.

I am the author of all my sorrows and pain and frustration.

I truly cannot believe I have been so spiritually blind.

It is so sick.

May 21, 1981

My walk with God is so odd right now. Extremely exciting within and non-eventful on the surface. Outwardly I feel no great spiritual feelings. Inside I know we're on the track.

May 28, 1981

My relationship with God has been sweet today and last night. I feel I will be getting a new commission from God very soon, and I am very excited and I think ready. Thank you my Lord. I am also very excited about the new baby on the way.

June 12, 1981

The Lord has shown me much the last week or so and I'm so grateful. My life's scripture is, "I buffet my body and make it my slave, lest possibly after preaching to others I myself should become disqualified." —Paul.

How grateful I am to Jesus and Paul.

June 19, 1981

[Keith has been disciplining himself a lot—getting up early, exercising—and he feels really good about it.]

Just got through putting most of my books on the shelf in my new office.

The euphoria of self-discipline is wearing off, but I don't care, it's the long-term benefits that are worth the struggle. As Catherine Booth says, "I don't care if I never live up to a holy life, I still will believe in it and preach it!" Of course she wanted to live it with all her heart and to a certain extent I believe she did.

So here I am six years later after conversion, still struggling with prayer and Bible study, but I believe if I make my body my slave, I will be able to control my wandering mind and unruly tongue.

June 26, 1981, New office

Wow, the Lord has been doing a work in our hearts. It's been such an incredible change.

We are being led into evangelism. It's amazing. The freedom and peace of my heart is what's so surprising. I knew that the Lord told me that this was a transition period, but I've never expected to go into full-on evangelism. I'm truly shocked!

I have a leading from the Lord to do an evangelistic album. This is the most excited I have been about a project in years and I fully need the wisdom and anointing from God. Please holy Lord, give me the secret of winning souls. I want to put it to music.

Dean Sherman spent the afternoon with me yesterday and really encouraged me to use my musical gift without embarrassment. I really believe that's what God is saying to me right now.

Oh there are doubts galore. How do you just turn your back on a previous message and calling? When you're sure you are through with your particular duty!

O Lord I wanna transfer so bad to the front lines! I want to see the lost, found!

July 3, 1981

Melody's due date is 9 days from today.

We are excited about the new baby. We're going to L.A. in July if it comes very soon. We're also planning on going to Art Katz's in Minnesota in August if the bus is fixed.

July 7, 1981

The Newsletter is going out only 7 weeks after the last one!!! What a victory! It's a little "color-crazy"!

Everything I felt the Lord saying about evangelism and recording is still not fully confirmed, but I believe it is the word of the Lord for me. Please Jesus show me the way and plant my feet firmly in You.

July 13, 1981

Yesterday was Melody's due date. No clear signs yet as to when. She's at the Dr.'s right now and she can literally come any minute. I have been so nervous and on edge about it. I am so excited! *[Rebekah was born 4 days later.]*

August 4, 1981

The children are blessing me so much. Bethany is getting so beautiful and Rebekah is just gorgeous. Josiah really is a light in our lives.

Jesus, I am so grateful for the healthy children you've given us, they didn't have to be so beautiful, but you made them that way. Bless You!

September 15, 1981

The kids are wonderful. Josiah's going to school. Bethany has become so cute and her and I are just beginning to develop a relationship. Rebekah is the most calm and joyful baby we've ever had—not to mention adorable! I am so grateful.

I finally got my "new" piano, the one from Fayetteville, Arkansas, a 9-foot Yamaha.

Last month I felt led to call Pastor Bob Wilhite in Fayetteville. I doubted and waited two days, but he prayed and agreed to give me his church piano if I'd replace it with a brand-new Yamaha, 9-foot. Thank you Jesus!

November 7, 1981, Saturday

I have been praying about the tours and albums and have been extremely hesitant about making any moves. Until two days ago I mistook these hesitancies as human fear, but the Lord showed me on Thursday that it was a fear of God in my heart that was having me wait. I now know that I can step out and book a spring East Coast tour, right after this Newsletter.

We are adding a beautiful, large room onto our house. Thank You Jesus and the ministry broke ground last Wednesday on our cafeteria/multipurpose building, and I do mean multi.

The children are beautiful, just gorgeous. I can't believe what lovely creatures God has put in our care and stewardship.

The Lord showed me that the whole agriculture thing was a big waste of time, and wholly not from Him, but He did not intervene, so I could get all those pipe dreams out of my system. I truly am being drained of all my personal private dreams and becoming quite ready for anything, void of desires for much else than what I already have. I have no thirsts for bigger and better things for me or the ministry, so I believe I'm ready to get a thirst for souls. Please Lord, put that thirst and burden for souls and disciples in my bosom.

Spiritually things could be a lot better but I'm trying to keep my ship from turning over through these stormy, stormy seas of life on earth as Christians. I am trying not to be so serious about ups and downs that I lose sight of the goal and like Peter end up in the drink. On the other hand, I don't want to be nonchalant and blind to the struggle either.

December 2, 1981

Just started working on a depressing song called "Good Things Don't Seem to Last" for the album to the lost.

My life and walk keep going up and down. I really feel ripped off by life.

Why did Adam fall? Why am I such an intense person? Why do I expect so much out of life?? Why can't I just be content with what God has given me? Why do I always feel there's something more?? Oh my heart aches because it knows not its Maker enough.

1982

January 17, 1982

I, Keith Green, have three natural-born children—Josiah David, Bethany Grace, and Rebekah Joy—and one adopted (not legally) daughter, Dawn. My wife Melody and I love and serve Jesus, and we need to accept ourselves and quit being condemned. I am very far from the way I know I should be, but I also know that God loves me and has been so patient with me. I am so miserable most of the time and yet God has provided and blessed me with so much—just like Solomon—and now I know that it's my job to learn to accept it and use it for His glory.

I am so "religioned" out. I am so weary of the struggle.

My weight is steadily on the rise. My prayer life is, as usual, very weak. My desires, as usual, are still lofty. It all seems like an endless merry-go-round. Yet I know there's an end to it all—death and judgment. If I were judged now, I would be judged a failure in my eyes—masquerading as a great man of God, running a great ministry. Yes, I have found much approval in men's eyes, but what about God's eyes? It seems He accepts me and loves me! I know He is not impressed with my works any more than He was with Solomon's. But I think He likes my heart. And if I will be judged on the motive and intent of my heart, then I'm okay. For out of a good heart must come good fruit.

O Lord help me accept myself as I am. Or help me change. I can't stand being this way and hating myself. I am <u>so</u> unhappy and uncontrolled!

<u>What's Happening?</u>

Mel and I have about 15 finished songs for the worship album. Bill Maxwell is coming next week to make final selections.

We, the ministry, are borrowing about $500,000 so we can finish the cafeteria/worship center, the airstrip, buy a big plane for the crusades, and build some dorms for the school and staff.

We almost sent out a financial appeal, but I didn't have peace about it, even though I had gotten counsel and the go-ahead from every direction, except my heart and spirit. We will just prayerfully pay the loans back.

The students arrived two days ago for the new school. We are all very excited about this new arm of our ministry. We just finished our fourth year of publishing the Newsletter.

January 20, 1982

Last night I spent about two hours with Dave Wilkerson and he shared his burden for me not to lose my "prophetic calling" and not to lose sight of the vision for revival worldwide. It was an inspiring talk and I was touched by the Holy Ghost.

Lord Jesus, I'm so grateful for all you've promised and all you are doing for us. I am so tired of being the center of attention. I truly want You to be the center of attention.

January 28, 1982

Leonard Ravenhill had a stroke last night. He couldn't talk or write for three hours. We're praying for him.

January 29, 1982

We visited Len at the hospital. He's having trouble talking. It's breaking his heart, but if he doesn't regain his speech perfectly I see the hand of God slowing him down to write and pray and reflect, but that's God's business, not mine.

Winkie is going to do half of the Spring Crusades with us, the other half I will do.

This morning I teach on "Devotion" at our school.

God has been so kind and patient with me, and now it's time to get serious about the call to serve Him. I've been so lax, undisciplined, and lazy. But I want so desperately to be true and faithful, this time something's got to change.

The Lord rebuked me yesterday for just occupying—just looking to do the next Newsletter, the next album and tour, etc. He showed me that my vision was far too small and that I had lost my pioneer spirit. I had hidden my talent of potential for revival and soul-winning in the ground. I had become a Corporate President instead of an apostle, making new territories available to God's Spirit to glorify Him.

Thank You for rebuking me in such love and kindness. I love You. Abba and Jesus.

February 10, 1982

Martin and I met for quite a while with the representative of Solna King Press about the future purchase of a Color King. It would run us over $200,000 but I know we're going to need it within a year if we grow like we did last time we were releasing albums and doing tours.

Then I taught a study on "What's Wrong with the Gospel?" part 1, for the Concert Crusade counselors. It was the strongest anointing I felt in over a year. How good it was to know that the Lord was there to bless and anoint after this whole year "in the desert" so to speak.

At home Melody reported to me that the Lord really used her to counsel a girl who'd been raped out of getting an abortion the next day. She was as ecstatic about being used by God as I was about the study. We both went to bed very happy Christians!

Somehow I feel that it would be more pleasing to God if I wasn't "doing my duty" at all, but I was madly in love with Him, constantly praying to Him and living off His Word. In fact I know this to be true, but I can't seem to "give up" my "devotional life." I am afraid that my soulish flesh will just take advantage of my leap of faith and turn me into a Word-less, prayer-less monster!

Please answer my questioning heart on this subject Lord Jesus. I want to know what pleases You and do it!

February 11, 1982

I'm starting to really feel the pressure of leaving for two weeks—in only two days. I must admit, I'm extremely nervous about this album. I'm always <u>so</u> insecure about the studio.

Spiritually things are a lot better now than the last few months. I'm still struggling with the whole "devotions" issue, but I won't give up even my "obligated times" until I have something better to replace them with.

April 5, 1982

It's been quite a while since I've written. I've done two crusades, an album, and one-and-a-half Newsletters. Yes, I've gotten quite a lot done. But spiritually I think I've been a failure. I've gained 10 pounds, a sure sign of backsliding for me, and I've been mostly disappointed by the so-called crusades. Mainly because I feel like I have no anointing. The worst part is that the audience doesn't even seem to notice. O God! Please give me a great big breaking and get me off my behind. I'm absolutely so numb to Your heart and burden. I can fool the world, but I can't fool my own conscience as to my stupid spiritual state.

There's nothing more sickening than to turn around and have to use the same methods you've despised for years. The silly altar call is all that seems to separate "the sheep from the audience." The (next day's) inquirers' meeting is a total failure. It seems that people just won't come. That's because there's not enough time (or anointing) to do the job supernaturally, so we've got to do it ourselves. Maybe I'm being too hard on myself, but that's how I feel in my heart. I feel like a complete idiot and a failure!

April 6, 1982

I can't believe how old I feel. There's an incredible amount of building and growth going on around here, but it's all so unexciting to me. I know that there's really only one thing that excites my soul and that's being close to Jesus. I must say that I've been closer to Him and I've also been quite a bit farther away too. But I know that He loves and cares for me. And that He really wants to use us to His greatest glory.

Melody and I really want to do a radio show beginning this coming year. It will either be a weekly show, or daily show, which I personally favor. It will include music, interviews, and topical discussions.

April 12, 1982

At Mobile, Alabama, things went horrible although they ended up good when God saved the day. I can boil it all down to my lack of brokenness before the Lord. There was a decent crowd, and the preparations were all together, but my heart was still crusted over from the months in L.A. without seeking God much. All I can say is that I have fallen away from a consecrated heart to the Lord. Onstage that night I felt the Lord desert me because of my lack of consecration and true devotion. I had not felt so terribly bad onstage since the last night at ORU three years ago. I finally cried out to God for help on stage, when my wandering mouth said some logically confusing things, and asked God for anointing and help—and He gave it. People gave their lives to Jesus and I knew that I needed to do something so I didn't keep blowing like that again.

Next day we flew to Nashville. About an hour before the concert started I went back to my hotel and cried my guts out before the Lord.

One thing that I asked God for in that prayer time was His heart. That's the only thing I needed from Him. The <u>only</u> thing. I told Him HE could have everything else, I'd turn over <u>everything</u> to Him if He'd just give me His Heart. Well that night's concert was one of the best I've ever had. The Word of God flowed out of my mouth in the smoothest way ever. I worshiped God and it didn't matter that there were even people there—it was God that I wanted to impress and bless and that's ALL!

The next day we had our last "next day meeting." The reason that it's the last one is because hardly anyone has been coming to anything but the concerts, so we're just going to have to make a big thing out of the "after concert meeting."

Lord Jesus please help me to stay hourly at Your side for the rest of my life. That is my only prayer! For if I stay at Your side, I have no need for anything else at all!!

Bless You my precious Lover!

April 13, 1982

My kids have been bringing me no limit of joy as I have been spending much more time with them than usual.

April 14, 1982

Tomorrow is the Houston Crusade and I'm not ready for it. I'm so sick of struggling, sometimes I just want to give up, but give up I won't! Please Jesus, don't let me slip down!!!

Well that's about that. I sure hope the Lord saves me from the fate of another concert without an anointing. I'll just die if I have to go out in front of a crowd again without His love and presence.

April 19, 1982

Well, this weekend went incredibly well. Traveling, praying, and ministering with John Dawson was one of the most rewarding and beautiful experiences I've ever been a part of—especially the praying!! I only hope and pray that someday God will teach me to pray with such fervency. I know it only comes with much time and prayer, practicing the principles of intercession. Lord, You see my heart has leapt because of this experience. Please lead me in this way—I know Your hand when I see it!

We got up and off to Houston on Thursday and I got a bit queasy on the way there. We slept for a while and then John showed up. After some time John and I prayed for the concert and he ended up prophesying some things to my heart from the Lord. They were beautiful, encouraging, and they bore fruit that proved they were truly from God.

We flew back here to sleep and then we flew out to Memphis on Friday morning. The concert went very smoothly and again John and I had an incredible time of prayer before the concert. We had over 100 inquirers (we'd had 200 in Houston!) and the meeting went well.

On Saturday, we flew to St. Louis and it was so refreshing to be out of the Bible Belt. That concert was one of the highlights of my whole life! I don't know why, but I get so turned on when there's a very large crowd—and there were about 9,500 people there that night—compared to about 3,400 the night before in Memphis. I only know that the message and music went more smoothly for me that night than in years. We had about 650 inquirers come forward and it took them about five whole minutes to file out of the hall. The inquirers themselves were the most broken of any concert. There were some real conversions, I believe.

We flew home in about 3 hours to our own strip. I flew up in the cockpit for a while and got even more of a desire to learn how to fly. Please Jesus, do not let me even start pilot's lessons unless You want me to. I realize that my own fleshly nature is not conducive to being a pilot, and that the devil would like to kill me if he could, but then again, if it's something You want me to do, I'll do it. I can truly see where it would benefit me both ways. I only want to do what God wants!

Please help us Lord to be and to do what You want from us. I want You to be in control of my soul with all my heart! I dearly praise and thank You for this past weekend and for the growing beautiful friendship with John Dawson. All praise and honor and glory be to You my sweetheart!

I played racquetball and I won, and felt kind of bad because I enjoyed winning (as usual) so much.

April 21, 1982

Yesterday I spent the morning with the kids.

May 3, 1982

Well, this past weekend was something else. We had 27,000 people come to the three concerts. About 600 came to the inquirers meetings and the offerings were <u>well</u> above the needs…

On Wednesday we left here about 6:00 PM for Indianapolis. It only took 3½ hours from our strip. What a blessing.

The next night 12,000 people came to the concert, and it was the biggest concert I've ever had. The inquirers' meeting was strange because we had to have it behind a curtain right there in the main hall, but under the circumstances things went as good as they could have.

On Friday we went to Peoria. The Lord showed a sense of humor by putting us in the fanciest hotel I've ever seen anywhere! (The one the night before was awful.) We had a great concert that night, 6,000 came to a hall that seated 7,000. We also had a great inquirers' meeting, but it was one of those strange nights where somebody tried to disrupt the meeting. A young girl said that she wanted to speak "a word from God," but she was obviously disturbed and I had to have her bodily removed off the stage twice! How embarrassing and unlovely—but it all worked out so smoothly. Most people didn't even notice it.

I listened to the new "Songs for the Shepherd" album and I wept and wept, as I heard what the Lord did on it. The songs' anointing was so powerful and they ministered to me in a way that none of my other albums ever could. Bill Maxwell was right when he said that God was doing something powerful in worship. He said that people were too beaten down by the world and the economy and all, and that worship was just the comfort they needed—not a bunch of "Jesus boogie." It's so amazing to me how the Lord stopped me dead in my tracks on doing the rock album, "Who Cares," and led me to do the worship one. Thank You my precious Savior! God is so wonderful!

May 5, 1982, Wednesday

I'm really trying to "buffet my body" so that I may be found ready when the Lord returns for me in His glory. I've never believed in the second coming so strongly, but then again, I've never had more trouble believing that it was going to happen very soon—so strongly. It's really hard to explain but I see a lot that has to be done on earth before the Lord returns and I pray that He lets me be a small part of it…(or even a BIG one!)

Buck and I played racquetball and he showed me a few pointers. He is such a sweet brother. I am so blessed that he and his family are living here.

May 9, 1982, Sunday

I got up at about 9:30 this morning and decided to try out church, so I went. Mel went with me and it was truly boring as usual. I just don't understand how people continue to go week after week! I don't want to be negative, but it just doesn't seem right. Church should be the most exciting time of the week, and the most exciting place on earth to believers!

May 11, 1982, Tuesday

Yesterday I was wondering what article I was supposed to write for the next Newsletter, and suddenly it came to me that God wanted me to do the "Prophets" article, so I decided to go over to Len's and bounce it off him. I told David Ravenhill, then he went home and told Len, and 5 minutes before I showed up at Len's, Len had been praying before the Lord and asking him to lead me to do that very article. When I got there to talk to him about it, he was still praying about it, so I took it as a definite confirmation that I was supposed to do the article.

Melody and I are really in love. We have so much to be grateful for, I was saying last night that the only thing we don't have that we need is a closer walk with God.

May 17, 1982

I feel that I'm finally ready to make a major growth move in Jesus. I think that I'm going to able to move out of this defeated place that I've been in for 7 years, and make some personal-growth headway—in my attitudes, in my family time, and in my walk with Jesus.

There are many things in the near future we are going to have to deal with. And I pray Jesus, that You will be right there in the cutting edge, helping, directing, protecting, and averting disaster and trouble!

June 23, 1982

Went out to dinner with some questionable businessmen who said they wanted to help a nearby ministry. It was okay, but I wasn't what they expected. I might have been too gritty and "human" for them. I think I'll have to get more like God so I don't stumble people anymore.

First of all Jesus I want to thank You for helping me get control of my mouth and stomach. I pray that You would help me get down to 170 pounds and stay there finally! That would be such a blessing.

Melody wrote a song called "Open Your Eyes," which really is beautiful and can be used on the "Who Cares" rock project. We also wrote a song together a few days ago called "Jesus Commands Us to Go!" which is very exciting for me.

Melody is a true inspiration and I'm so grateful to Jesus for that wife of mine.

July 8, 1982

The computers have been down for almost 10 days, but I was in L.A. for about a week of that time. The time there was precious, mainly because of the time we spent with different people like Loren Cunningham and Ralph Winter. We also saw lots of friends.

Saturday the festival at Devonshire Downs was okay, though the attendance was sparse. But the evening service with Loren and me went very well. Many people responded to our dual "missions" message. We were very much in harmony. Afterwards we spent some time ministering to a guy I knew from the Bla Bla days who had been cracked up in a motorcycle accident.

On Sunday we went to our little one-week beach rental. Mel, Dawn, and I went to see the new Star Trek movie that night and it thoroughly entertained and inspired me. In fact the main theme from the movie, "the needs of the many outweigh the needs of the few," really hit me hard, and was instrumental in my benefit concert on Monday for the Youth With A Mission mercy ship.

The meeting with Loren and his wife, Darlene, lasted till after midnight. It was extremely precious. They shared their vision and ministry with us and we shared our need in vision and heart with them. I can't remember a more exciting evening in a long time.

The next morning, they got up, fellowshipped, prayed, and went on their way. I spent the late afternoon playing with the kids near the water on the sand.

On Friday Ralph Winter came out for a meeting on missions. Later in the evening my folks showed up to spend the night.

July 11, 1982

Today I'm going to take the kids swimming at YWAM lake. They need a nice day with their daddy. Thank You for these precious kiddies, Jesus. I have <u>so</u> much.

July 22, 1982, 2:00 PM

We went to that YWAM camp in Colorado and had a great time. The family and I caught about 120 trout. We had some good family fellowship and I can definitely say that I had my vacation. We left for there on Monday and came back late Friday night. Since then we have found out that <u>Melody is pregnant!</u> Thank You Father, I truly pray this child is healthy!!

On Monday, Melody's back was awful, so I flew to the Christian Booksellers Convention in Dallas with just Josiah. I saw a whole lot of people I hadn't seen in a long while including the Talbot brothers.

There's a whole lot of people coming to visit us over the next month. John Smalley and his whole family from the early Vineyard days are coming next week. Amidst all this I have to do the next Newsletter, which is on the subject of missions, and keep the ministry on an even financial and spiritual keel. Please Father I need Your help. I am in great need of wisdom beyond my years and ability that can come only from Your throne.

Well, all in all things are going extremely well. God is truly watching out for us in <u>every</u> way. People are coming to join us and finances are holding their own, and our family is doing very well. We have been so blessed by Jesus and we're so grateful. Please help us in the weeks ahead to keep our priorities straight. We need to have a continual touch from You.

Today I went to work on my missions article. Please help me redeem my time!

[On July 28, 1982 John and DeDe Smalley arrived. They had promised their six children an airplane ride. Keith took Josiah and Bethany along, and 20 seconds after takeoff the plane crashed and exploded on impact. Everyone on board went to be with Jesus, including Don Burmeister, the ministry pilot.]

The Concert
Messages

A Word from Melody About Keith's Concert Messages

If you've only heard Keith's music, but never had the chance to be at one of his concerts, you've only met half of the man. Heard half of his heart. When Keith began doing Christian concerts, he always delivered compelling messages between songs. I guess some would call it preaching—and it was some of the most powerful preaching I've ever heard! Keith's words were always passionate, direct, and straight from his heart. His primary motivation for every concert was to see Jesus glorified, lives changed, and souls won.

Keith always used his concerts to challenge believers to live the life they said they believed in, and he included the gospel message for anyone who didn't know Jesus. Keith was intense, deep, and focused during his concerts—but many were surprised to find he had such a great sense of humor too. He created and acted out funny and often edgy modern-day parables—playing every role, changing voices, and jumping around the stage, just to drive home an idea. Keith kept a loose concert agenda, always searching for the Holy Spirit's plan for the specific needs of the people there. At the end of each concert, Keith gave believers and unbelievers a chance to respond to the Lord. This was a big change from Keith's pre-teen years, when he simply wanted to perform...to captivate and entertain an audience.

Keith was a songwriter, musician, and actor. At age 11, he was the youngest member of the American Society of Composers, Authors and Publishers (ASCAP). That same year, Keith was also signed to a recording contract that led to the release of his first single, called "Cheese and Crackers." Keith grew up doing concerts, being on TV, and acting in live theater. Then in his mid-teens Keith began to feel that his music could have a higher meaning. He wanted to help people by bringing them an inspiring message. When he met Jesus at 21, it all came into focus. His message changed too. Now Keith knew his call. God really did want to use his music for a much greater end—as a tool to transform lives.

Keith called himself a music minister, never a performer. In concert, he often wore a custom-lettered T-shirt saying "Jesus Is The Only Star" to make his point. Still, sometimes Keith was given the praise he knew belonged only to God, which grieved him deeply. Some people assume that when someone is onstage he is "better" or "more spiritual" than he really is. But Keith knew that only God's grace allowed him to be used. Keith spoke against the Christian "celebrity culture" he saw. This culture made it difficult for him (and other ministers) to just go to church on Sunday to receive something from God as any other believer would want to do. Still, he could never be just a "regular" Christian in the eyes of some who insisted on putting him on a pedestal. He didn't want the praise, he just wanted people to praise the One who was using him. Keith was very grateful for God's favor and excited that people came to his concerts to hear his music—but above all, he wanted them to hear from Jesus.

And they did.

Keith sang and preached in prisons, on military bases, in parks and churches, at the beach, and in some of the largest stadiums in America. Countless thousands came to the Lord, rededicated their lives to God, went into missions, and decided to use their talents for God's service. It is so wonderful that Keith's music and writings are still changing lives today. Although Keith carefully kept a personal journal, there were only a few concerts he went out of his way to have recorded. Still many other people recorded them and later sent them to me. We've selected some of the best concert messages from those tapes to share with you.

Today, Keith's words are just as relevant as the day he spoke them—and they will bless, inspire, and challenge you on your journey of getting closer to Jesus. I know Keith would be amazed to see how God has continued to use his few years of ministry and multiply them into this new millennium and into the hearts of a whole new generation.

When Keith went to be with Jesus just seven years after meeting Him, the Lord gave me John 12:24—about a grain of wheat needing to die in order to bear much fruit. I understood it to mean that God was going to take what He had put into Keith's heart and, like seed, scatter it across the land into the hearts of many. I pray that these concert messages will inspire you to rise up and cry out to God for grace and growth in your own life—and for the lost, the poor, and the hurting.

Perhaps it's time to let your voice be heard.

Melody Green
October 2001

1   What Jesus Said About Himself

*I am the way and the truth and the life. No one comes
to the Father except through me.*

—JOHN 14:6

When I was searching for the Lord, I'd ask Buddhists what they thought about Jesus Christ, and they'd claim that He was a Buddha. I'd ask the Krishnas, and they'd tell me Jesus was the incarnation of God for His age. The Maharishi said that we could all attain to the same spiritual level as Jesus. Yogananda claimed that he had "Christ-consciousness." Even rabbis told me that Jesus was a good man who just got off track somewhere along the way. *Nobody* had anything bad to say about Jesus. No one ever said that He was an idiot or a liar—He was just a nice teacher or He just one of many ways to get to God.

Finally I decided I'd read the Bible for myself to see what Jesus said about Himself. I soon discovered that looking for truth in the Bible is a dangerous thing to do. Don't ever read the Bible unless you're prepared to respond to the truth you'll find there.

When I got to John 14, I read something that scared me. Here was Jesus Christ saying, "I am the way." Everyone else had been telling me that Jesus was *one* of the ways. Then I read on and Jesus said, "I am the truth." My mind responded with, "No, Jesus. What You really mean is that You *know* the truth, right?"

Then Jesus said He was "the life." Okay, I thought, I can go for that one. But then I read on, finishing the verse: "No one comes to the Father except through me." *Uh, Jesus,* I thought, *why are You being so narrow-minded here? I mean, all these other guys—Buddha, Muhammad—they've given You some recognition. Why do You say that nobody gets to God except through You? Are You on some kind of ego trip?* I was really mad at Jesus for His narrow-mindedness.

Then I turned back to John 10, where I had read something else I didn't understand. There Jesus had said that unless we enter by "the door" we can't get in. He said that only thieves and robbers try to get in by any other way. The disciples didn't get what Jesus was trying to say, so He had to spell it out for them. He said, "I am the door. If anyone enters by me, he will be saved, and will go in and out and find pasture."

Wow. Jesus is the *door*. And Jesus is the *way*, the *truth*, and the *life*. I understood it, but I couldn't quite accept it...yet. For another two years I prayed, "Jesus, if You really are the only way, You're going to have to show me." I was really into the idea of "gurus," so I prayed, "Jesus, if You really are *the* guru, show me. Come into my heart."

As a result of that prayer, things started to happen in my life. Jesus Christ proved Himself to me. My old friends began to say, "Keith's blown it. He's flipped out." At first, their words bothered me, but then I realized that all Jesus' friends thought He'd flipped out too. His mother and brothers even came to take Him away.

Unless you swallow your pride, open your heart, and say, "Okay, if You're there, please come into my life," nothing anyone will ever say will prove Jesus to you. He has to do it Himself. I'm not talking about going to church—I'm talking about having Him get into you and you getting into Him in such a way that you're a walking, living church.

2

Hyprocisy

Putting aside all malice and all deceit and hypocrisy…
—1 Peter 2:1 NASB

When I travel to give my concerts, I get a view of the modern-day American Christian church that most people never see. If you're a Baptist minister, you travel the Baptist circuit. If you're an Assembly of God minister, you travel the Assembly of God circuit. But I travel all the circuits. I've played in every denominational church I can think of, and as a result, I've discovered what the world hates most about Christianity: Christians.

It would be okay if they hated us for the right reasons—if they hated us because of our love and our joy and our good deeds. But the problem is, they hate us for our hypocrisy. Meanwhile we're thinking that unbelievers resent our good works. We don't like to admit to our hypocrisy. We don't like to admit that the world is tired of hearing us say "praise the Lord." They're tired of seeing the bumper stickers without seeing something Christlike going on inside of the car. They're tired of our T-shirt philosophy and our rings and our necklaces and our phoniness. They're hungry and thirsty for truth. They want to see Christians being Christians, or else to them, we're just another trip.

In my neighborhood I'd rather have my neighbors know that I'm a Christian by how I live than have 4 million people who don't know me buy my albums. If I'm not a Christian at home, woe unto me if I try to be one on the road.

I've seen that in every city there's a remnant of right-on, on-fire, true believers—and there are also a lot of pew-warmers. But if God wanted pew-warmers, He'd just set a bunch of hot-water bottles on the pews. They'd have about the same attention span, and they'd cool off as quickly too—and they're made out of plastic.

If you're a pew-warmer, I'm not telling you you're doomed. I'm telling you you're dooming others. I'm not telling you you're hell-bound. I'm telling you you're sleeping while others are sinking down into a fiery eternity.

Unbelievers are looking to us to show them the love of God. But today the church uses the word "love" as some kind of invisible, ethereal kind of myth. True love isn't a myth. I've seen it often, but not often enough. Instead what I've seen more often in churches today is a counterfeit love that is couched in phrases like "How are you doing today?" or "It's so good to see you." But in reality on the way to church the conversation was more like, "I hope the sermon's short today. I want to watch the football game this afternoon," or "I hate that orange lipstick you're wearing," or "Sit down, shut up, and stop pulling your brother's hair," or "Hurry up to Sunday school; you're late." Then they walk in the church doors with a "hallelujah" on their lips.

Guys, we're in a sorry, sorry mess. The world is sick of it and God is sick of it. It's enough to make Him vomit, according to Revelation 3:16.

What I'm saying is this: We better get steamy hot as Christians. We could take a lesson from Paul. Wherever he traveled the result was either revival or riot. When was the last time your witness caused a riot? You answer, "Keith, I don't feel called to a riot ministry."

Okay then, when was the last time your witness caused a revival?

3

Scriptures Never Used in Greeting Cards

Many of his disciples said, "This is a hard teaching.
Who can accept it?"

—JOHN 6:60

Have you ever noticed the verses in the Bible that the pastors and preachers don't want to talk about? We all the know the popular verses like John 3:16, or "Fear not, little flock, it's the Father's good pleasure to give you the kingdom." These kinds of verses get preached on all the time. But these verses alone can lead to an easy armchair Christianity. But what about the verses that you never hear preached on? The hair-raising stuff like, "Many are called, but few are chosen," or "He who endures to the end shall be saved." About the former, people say, "Well, I know I'm chosen, so I don't have to worry about that." Or about the latter they'll say, "You've got to understand about the dispensations of God to understand what Jesus really means."

But let me tell you, Jesus is coming back and a lot of Christians are going to be surprised. The Bible says that day will come "like a thief in the night." But it goes on to say that we should be awake, watching, vigilant.

Many Christians, including me sometimes, walk around with a chip on our shoulder that seems to say, "Well, I'm saved and I know it. I'm waiting for the Rapture when I'll go to be with Christ and all you unbelievers will be left behind." Our faith is centered totally on ourselves and all we get from it. We're like a 200-pound baby in our crib with a big bottle. We get fatter and fatter, but spiritually we're really getting leaner and leaner, only we don't really know it. We have no substance.

But if we really want to see what God thinks of our spiritual depth, we can listen to what James tells us: True religion before

God is visiting the widows and orphans in their affliction and to keep oneself unspotted from the world. Then someone will say, "Keith, I don't feel like I have a widow-and-orphan ministry. I feel like God wants me to work with the people in Beverly Hills. And I really have a burden for Maui too."

Really?! Sometimes I wonder about our generation of Christians. I wonder if perhaps we aren't the most selfish "bless me" generation that has ever walked the earth.

I wonder and I shudder at the answer.

4   Compare Yourself to Jesus

We are not bold to class or compare ourselves with some of those who commend themselves; but when they measure themselves by themselves and compare themselves with themselves, they are without understanding.

—2 CORINTHIANS 10:12 NASB

When I first became a Christian it was easy for me to just relax and entertain an audience. After all, I had been playing at cafés, nightclubs, and colleges for a long time. I just changed venues. I could play at a church and get them boogying just as easily as before. I know how to entertain. I know how to get people going. But after a while my goal became to get people changing. But before a life can change, a person has to see the need to change. Before you get a tooth filled, you have to admit to having a cavity. You won't get rid of the toothache by walking around saying, "Oh, it's nothing. Just a swollen gland. It's okay."

Before you turn a light on, you have to admit to darkness. Before you can get on fire for the Lord, you have to admit you're lukewarm. Before you're broken by God, you need to admit you're hard.

The problem is, most of us compare ourselves to other Christians. It's not hard to find another Christian who's as lukewarm as we are. It's like a seedling planted in a grove of miniature trees. Although it's tiny, it looks around at the other little trees and thinks, "Wow, I've gotta grow so I can be taller like the others." Just then a logging truck speeds by. The baby tree gasps, "Is that a tree?"

If we compare ourselves to other Christians, we'll be totally deceived. We'll always find someone we are doing better than—and we'll always find someone who's doing better than we are. But if we compare ourselves to Jesus, we'll never stop growing. Jesus is our ultimate role model.

5   Love the Poor Like God Does

All they asked was that we should continue to remember the poor, the very thing I was eager to do.
                                    —GALATIANS 2:10

One third of the world's population goes to bed every night having eaten the equivalent of a half a cup of rice or less all day. That's 1.3 *billion* people.

In America, we go to bed with full stomachs and maybe a brief, "Thank You, Lord."

There's nothing wrong with full stomachs—but *every* person on the planet deserves enough food to eat each day. Our richness should spur us to a greater responsibility—especially those of us who are Christians. God calls us to share our abundance with those who don't have enough. This isn't a suggestion from God, nor even a request, but an imperative. A command.

In addition to our abundance of food, we're also blessed spiritually. We have freedom to share the gospel with others who are in spiritual poverty. But what do we do with these incredible spiritual opportunities? Do we readily share with others—or do we let each golden opportunity slip by? Do we spend our time and money on ourselves or do we invest it in the kingdom of God by allowing it to bless others? Do we spend *ourselves* on our interests, or do we invest our lives in the work of Christ?

If every person changed just one person tomorrow, and *they* changed one person the next day, within eight months everybody on the planet would be changed. If you led just one person to the Lord each day and they went out and did the same, within eight months the whole world could be saved. Sadly, leading the average person to the Lord today and putting him in the average church is like giving birth to a baby and throwing him in the freezer. We've got to do something to change this. And here's what we can do:

We can allow Jesus to put a heart of fire in us. Not a bad kind of fire, but the good kind. A warm purifying fire that burns up everything that shouldn't be there. When a goldsmith puts gold in the fire, it burns away the dross. That's how they turn 18-karat gold into 24-karat gold—they burn away the impurities. Ten-karat gold is real impure. It needs the heat to purify it, to make it more valuable, more precious.

If you want to be a man or woman who is used of God, valuable in God's service, let Him burn away the dross. That happens by turning everything in your life over to Him. Hold nothing back. Let Him use you for a change, instead of you using Him.

6   Death Comes to Every Door

He will die for lack of instruction, and in the greatness
of his folly he will go astray.

—Proverbs 5:23 NASB

What does your life consist of? Do you get up every morning, brush your teeth, go to work, come home, watch Monday-night football, go to bed, and start all over again the next morning? And you keep doing this until you make enough money to buy your grave plot at Forest Lawn and then you die? If so, that's no life, that's barely an existence.

The other day I was listening to the news and the reporter said, "Today we're going to look into the high cost of dying." And I thought, *Right. Die before Tuesday and we'll give you a 20 percent discount.* It was pretty disgusting. They were talking about death as if they were selling toothpaste. Hey, did you know you can get a solid aluminum casket—on sale *now!*

I don't understand it. We all have this one thing in common: We're gonna die. And yet we treat our death as either a business opportunity or we're in denial that it will happen to us. As I get closer to the Lord, the more it blows my mind that people are so oblivious to eternity. I drive down the street, and I see people just going through the motions of their life as if to say, "I'm not gonna die. There's no God, or if there is, He doesn't care how I live." So they push their impending death out of their minds and chase the dollar or sex or big houses or a better job. Some chase nature or even spiritual ideals. But the one thing they won't chase is Jesus. It's really weird to watch these people. It's as if they're all hypnotized. I was like that too at one time. Then the Lord snapped me out of it.

As I drive along, I find myself with a deep compassion for these hypnotized people. I pray through the tears, "God, reveal Yourself to these people. Open their eyes!"

You were once like these people and so was I. But then I came out of the trance the world is in and became aware of my own mortality. I realized I'm going to die someday. You're going to die someday too. When God graciously snaps us out of our sleep and allows us to see the finiteness of our days on earth, we see things from a different perspective. We can forget that plot in Forest Lawn. Monday-night football loses its glamour. Our lives become focused on an eternity with God. When we're fully ready to die, only then are we really prepared to live as we should.

Our gospel did not come to you in word only, but also in power and in the Holy Spirit and with full conviction.

—1 Thessalonians 1:5 nasb

If the Holy Spirit left the churches in your town, would you even notice a difference? How could you tell? Would the church programs stop? Would the services change? Would the youth group be any different? How about the singles group? Or the Christian concerts? What about the spaghetti feed? Could a slick evangelist still bring people down the aisle through guilt? Could a persuasive pastor still get big offerings to pay for the stained glass windows and the organs and the buses? Could a sly charismatic still speak in tongues anytime he wanted to? Could a fundamentalist Baptist still quote his scriptures just as well?

It seems we don't need the Holy Spirit in our churches anymore. We've got everything we need to make the machinery run smoothly. But look at our individual lives. I don't know about you, but I've never needed the Holy Spirit in my life more than I do now. I need Him to supply my every need, hour by hour, minute by minute.

God desires to bring true Holy Spirit–led revival to every city, to every church, including yours. The Holy Spirit wants to be so evident in the churches that if He suddenly leaves, everything would change and everyone would notice. The path to this kind of revival is through repentance and humility. Repentance from our hypocrisy and humility in that we recognize that we can do nothing apart from Him.

Without this kind of revival, we can kiss our cities, our states, and our nation good-bye. Judgment will come to this land. There will come a time when being a Christian will cost you your life. Nobody wants to hear this message. No one wants to believe that our nation has lost its moral fiber.

More than ever, in the midst of our decay, God calls us to take a stand for holiness, righteousness, and faith in the midst of a perverse generation. More than ever God calls us to pray for our families, our cities, our country, our churches, our pastors, our elders.

Get down on your face and let the rivers pour out of your eyes and repentance pour out of your heart. Get before the throne of God and intercede. Grab hold of God and implore Him to sweep through our land with revival—true revival, not that which is dreamed up in the heart of man.

If we pray, God will hear. But *will* we pray?

8   Conviction vs. Condemnation

Draw near to God and He will draw near to you.

—James 4:8 NASB

We all have areas of our life that need cleaning up. Some of us still have restitution to make from before we were Christians. Some of us from *after* we became Christians. To walk strongly with God, we must have a clear conscience about our past—and about our present.

Do you have a clear conscience? Have you murdered anyone in your heart?

Try this: Shut your eyes and think about the word "bitterness." Look at the face that comes to mind. You've murdered that person in your heart. Here's another word to think about with your eyes closed: "Lust." Does the face of someone come to mind—someone with whom you've committed adultery or fornication through sexual fantasy? Jesus said that to indulge the fantasy was as serious as committing the deed.

We know that the church of God, the bride of Christ, is spotless. We know that we're seated in the heavenlies with Him. In that sense, we're already clean. But when we look at what remains in our heart, we have to confess that we're unclean. I, Keith Green, know that I'm a wretch. I need to clean up my act through the grace that Jesus supplies. If I don't, God won't use me. Nor will I have that clear conscience that gives me the peace of God.

We have a promise: "Draw near to God and He will draw near to you." In the nearness of God we find the power to change, the grace to live, and the blessings of a clear conscience. Don't waste another day without making things right with those you've wronged, including God.

Remember that though God will convict us of our sins, Satan will try to condemn us. But don't worry—get rid of the things that God is convicting you of and Satan will have no power to condemn. He can only get a foothold in areas that aren't right. There's no condemnation to those that are in Christ Jesus.

Just make sure you're in Christ Jesus.

9   Our Praise Opens the Heavens

Let everything that has breath praise the LORD. *Praise the* LORD.

—PSALM 150:6

Most of the songs I've written have been for the Lord. But one day the Lord gave me a song that was from Him to *me*. It came about when I was complaining, "Lord, what's the matter? You haven't given me any new songs in a long time." He said, "Keith, I have a bagful of songs for you. You haven't taken the time to sit at your piano in the right frame of mind to receive them." Just then Melody came in and gave me a note from the Lord that said, "Just sit still and I'll give you a song."

Melody didn't know the depth of what I had been going through, so it was really amazing for her to confirm what the Lord had been telling me. So I sat still, and the Lord gave me this song that was birthed from a song Melody had begun a few days before. It explains why God is so desirous of communion with us. He knows that our only true happiness is in worshiping Him. Some Christians mistakenly think of worship as long-faced, white-robed, dirge-singing saints. But worshiping from God's point of view really means putting Him first, second, third, and last. It means putting ourselves totally aside. It means that we become as nothing and give Him the right to be everything in our life.

It's the most incredible feeling to be praying to God and realize that He's looking at you and everything He sees is *His*. He gives it back to us, but only as stewards of His possessions.

It was then that He gave me this song:

When I Hear the Praises Start

My son, My son
Why are you striving?
You can't add one thing
To what's been done for you.
I did it all while I was dying.
Rest in your faith
My peace will come to you.

For when I hear the praises start,
I wanna rain upon you
Blessings that will fill your heart.
I see no stain upon you
Because you are My child
And you know Me
To Me you're only holy,
Nothing that you've done remains,
Only what you do for Me.

My child, My child
Why are you weeping?
You will not have to wait forever.
That day and that hour is in My keeping
The day I'll bring you into heaven.

For when I hear the praises start,
My child, I wanna rain upon you
Blessings that will fill your heart.
I see no stain upon you
Because you are My child
And you know Me.
To Me you're only holy,
Nothing that you've done remains,
Only what you do in Me.

My precious bride,
The day is nearing
When I'll take you in My arms and hold you.

I know there's so many things
That you've been hearing.
But you just hold on
To what I've told you.

For when I hear the praises start,
My bride, I wanna rain upon you
Blessings that will fill your heart.
I see no stain upon you
Because you are My child,
And you know Me
To me you're only holy,
Nothing that you've done will remain,
Only what you do for Me.

*...the serpent of old who is called the devil and Satan,
who deceives the whole world; he was thrown down to
the earth, and his angels were thrown down with him.*
—REVELATION 12:9 NASB

Satan's greatest trick is to make people believe he doesn't exist. He goes around with football cleats three inches long, bashing anyone in the head who will listen to his message, "There's no devil."

But once we wake up and realize that the devil exists, the temptation is to focus more on the devil than on Jesus. That's how Satan will keep digging those cleats into believers—by getting them to be preoccupied with him. All we really need to do with Satan is expose him to Jesus. Utter a "praise the Lord" in his direction and he's gone.

The devil is really a coward when it comes to Jesus. The only thing Satan fears is Jesus Christ. And the only thing about a believer he fears is Jesus Christ *in* the believer. If you don't have Jesus in you, he's not afraid of you at all. And if you don't believe in Satan, he has won the battle for your heart.

No One Believes in Me Anymore

(Satan's Boast)

Oh, my job keeps gettin' easier
As time keeps slippin' away.
I can imitate the brightest light
And make your night look just like day.
I put some truth in every lie
To tickle itchin' ears

You know I'm drawin' people just like flies
'Cause they like what they hear.
I'm gainin' power by the hour,
They're falling by the score.
You know, it's gettin' very simple now
Since no one believes in me anymore.

Oh, heaven's just a state of mind
My books read on your shelf.
And have you heard that God is dead?
I made that one up myself!
They're dabblin' in magic spells,
They get their fortunes read,
They heard the truth but turned away
And followed me instead…

I used to have to sneak around,
But now they just open their doors,
You know, no one's watching for my tricks
Because no one believes in me anymore.

Everyone likes a winner.
With my help you're guaranteed to win.
Hey, man, you ain't no sinner, no!
You've got the truth within,

And as your life slips by you believe the lie
That you did it on your own,
But I'll be there to help you share
Our dark eternal home.

Oh, my job keeps getting easier,
As day slips into day,
The magazines, the newspapers,
Print every word I say.
This world is just my spinning top,
It's all like child's play.
You know, I dream that it will never stop,
But I know it's not that way.

Still my work goes on and on,

Always stronger than before,
I'm gonna make it dark before the dawn
Since no one believes in me anymore.

Well now I used to have to sneak around,
But now they just open their doors.
You know, no one watches for my tricks
Since no one believes in me anymore,
Well I'm gaining power by the hour,
They're falling by the score,
You know, it's getting very easy now
Since no one believes in me anymore.
No one believes in me anymore,
No one believes in me anymore.

When you pray, you are not to be like the hypocrites;
for they love to stand and pray in the synagogues and
on the street corners so that they may be seen by men.
Truly I say to you, they have their reward in full.

—MATTHEW 6:5 NASB

Has this ever happened to you: You've got everything in your life under control. Everything's going great. You're reading your Bible every day, you're getting good fellowship with the brothers and the sisters, and your prayer life is really powerful. And then seemingly all of a sudden you notice that you're starting to strive spiritually. When you pray in front of others, you close your eyes a little tighter. You pepper your speech with a few extra "praise the Lords" or "hallelujahs." Maybe you stand on your tiptoes and rock a bit when you pray. Others look at you and think, *Wow, he must be really spiritual!*

But we know what's really happening, don't we? We're starting to get religious. We're no longer resting in what Christ has done, so we begin to strive in our spiritual flesh. We give out that extra little grunt when we pray or we start speaking in a voice with that special spiritual tremolooooo.

Brethren, we need to lay our striving down. When I was feeling so "spiritual" in my flesh, the Lord said, "Keith, the only way I'm really satisfied with you is when I see you *in Christ,* not in your flesh. What I want from you is the praises of your heart. Not your fleshly striving."

Don't worry about letting people know how spiritual you are. Instead, "let your light so shine before men that they praise your Father in heaven." True spirituality isn't about us and what we do. It's about Him and what He did for us.

*The LORD will guide you always; he will satisfy your
needs in a sun-scorched land and will strengthen your
frame. You will be like a well-watered garden, like a
spring whose waters never fail.*

—ISAIAH 58:11

Some days our walk with God seems dry. We look around and wonder what our life is all about. That's when we need to think about our future with God. We need to remember our destination is a place where there is no time, except eternity. We'll sit at the feet of Jesus and He will answer all our questions. Then we'll get up and go for lunch, munching on the latest crop from the Tree of Life.

Folks, God is so good. For us, this present world is the only hell we'll ever know. For unbelievers, this earth is the only heaven they'll ever know, because earth is heaven compared to hell, and it's hell compared to heaven. The thing is, we don't need to wait until we die to experience a taste of heaven. We have the Holy Spirit in us, sort of like a down payment on eternity. He gives us that foretaste of all that's ahead for us.

When you feel dry, remember He is now, and always will be, our Living Water. Drink freely, brothers. Splash around the joy, sisters. This is our heritage.

13   The Truth Is Not a Cliché

Amazed and perplexed, they asked one another, "What does this mean?" Some, however, made fun of them and said, "They have had too much wine."

—ACTS 2:12,13

Before I became a Christian it used to bug me when I'd hear "praise the Lord." I'd say with disgust, "What's this 'praise the Lord' stuff anyway? Why do these simpleminded Christians always say the same thing?" It just didn't make sense to me. It sounded like a cliché.

It reminded me of my dad. Whenever he came home, he'd say to my mom, "I love you." I thought to myself, *He's been saying that same thing for 30 years. Enough already!*

But one day it hit me: He means it. When my dad says that same old phrase to my mom, it may seem like a cliché to me, but to them those words have a lot of meaning. Later, as a Christian I realized that if you don't know the Lord, "praise the Lord" *is* just a cliché. But if you know the Lord you're praising, it's reality. The words are full of meaning—if you really mean them. If you tell someone you love them four million times, it's still not a cliché if you really love them.

The Christian's intense happiness is something that non-Christians just can't understand. They don't like Christians because of the ear-to-ear smiles and the joy they have while traveling through a world filled with despair.

One evening Matthew Ward and I went into a donut shop. We were full of God's joy and weren't afraid to express it. Especially Matthew—he's usually bouncing around with the joy of the Lord. The lady behind the counter said, "I don't usually get anyone in here loaded until at least 7:30."

Matthew looked at me and said, "She thinks we're stoned!"

I grinned at the lady and said, "Lady, we're loaded with the Holy Spirit!"

She got real quiet and just said, "Uh, you boys want to take your donuts?"

Sometime later I was in the church restroom after a service, praising God. Yes, it's all right—you can even praise God in the bathroom. I was getting ministered to by the graffiti on the walls—you know, John 3:16, stuff like that. It was really kind of funny. The joy of the Lord comes on us in the strangest places. In that bathroom, being ministered to by the Lord, I wrote a song that expresses the joy God gives to every Christian.

Thank You Jesus

Thank You Jesus,
For what You're doing for me,
Thank You Jesus,
I want the whole world to see,
That You're not just a picture
On the wall in my room,
That You're faster than lightning,
And You're coming back soon!

Thank You Jesus,
For all the good things You do,
Thank You Jesus,
I wish they all could know You,
That You're not just a book
Collecting dust on the shelf,
And if they don't want to read it,
You're gonna be back to tell them Yourself.

Well, I don't understand
Why my fellowman

Had to turn away,
From all the good things that You say
They're still trying to find a better way
But You know they won't
(Unless they invent one, then we'll have to patent it.)

Thank You Jesus
For all the good things You've done
Thank You Jesus
I really want to tell You Lord
I'm having so much fun
Loving You.

Thank You Jesus
For this here smile on my face
Thank You Jesus
I really want to shout it to the whole human race
That You're not just this building
On the corner where we meet
They can know You in person
You're a pleasure to meet.

Thank You Jesus, Oh thank You Jesus
Thank You Jesus, I only want to thank You Jesus

I don't care what they say
They're gonna call You a cliché
I'm gonna love You anyway!

14 Both Spirit and Word Are Needed

The letter kills, but the Spirit gives life.

—2 CORINTHIANS 3:6

It's so beautiful to see the right balance between the teaching of the Word and the exercising of spiritual gifts. Sometimes believers feed on the meat of the Word—and as important as that is— they don't have the Spirit to act as a balance. So what happens? People who are fed on the Word without the Spirit get spiritually constipated. There's no roughage. There's no way for the Word to be put into action without the Spirit.

On the other hand, there are some Christians who are so obsessed with the gifts, they don't even read their Bibles. The extent of their Christian life is speaking in tongues or jumping and rolling around on the floor. This isn't God's way either. Both camps, the Word without the Spirit and the Spirit without the Word, are suffering from a serious deficiency. The result is spiritual infirmity. Disease. Suffering and everything else that accompanies sickness.

But then there are Christians who have the right balance. They feast on a diet that includes large doses of the Word applied to their hearts by the Holy Spirit of God. These people don't suffer from deficiencies. They stay spiritually healthy and strong.

What's your life like? Are you dry from lack of the water of the Spirit? Or are you starving because you don't feast on the meat of the Word? Find the right balance and stay strong.

15   In Unity We Will Prevail

*Now I exhort you, brethren, by the name of our Lord
Jesus Christ, that you all agree and that there be no
divisions among you, but that you be made complete
in the same mind and in the same judgment.*

—1 CORINTHIANS 1:10 NASB

If you drive down the main street of almost any town in
America, you'll see several different kinds of churches. In some
towns, you'll see a *lot* of different churches, all of which profess
Christianity. And if these churches ever seriously got together
for the Lord, can you imagine the spiritual power that could be
unleashed?

But so often such unity—the kind God desires—is impossible
because we want to fellowship around our doctrines, around our
differences rather than around Jesus. We may agree on the
basics—the virgin birth, the resurrection, the need to tell others
about Christ, the return of Christ, but beyond these basics we
start to form schisms around our pet doctrines. We get into pre-
trib, post-trib, mid-trib, no trib, pan-millennial, post-millennial,
and so on. Then you get "Can a Christian have a demon?" or
"Can you lose your salvation?" or "Do you speak in tongues?" and
so on.

What Christian hasn't had discussions with other believers
about these issues? We all have our opinions, but too often we
fellowship around our opinions of Christ, rather than Christ
Himself. Brethren, these are the last days and this kind of division must stop. When you find yourself dividing over doctrinal
disputes, simply get off the subject and talk about the goodness
of God and the grace He's shown us in Christ. We may only have
a short time left until the Lord returns. And even if He doesn't

return for a long time, He's going to return at the end of each one of our lives for each of us.

It's not important that we convert people so that they come to our church. What is the church anyway—is it the building where we gather? No. *We* are the church. And when someone is born again they too are incorporated into the Body of Christ, no matter which local body of believers they choose to fellowship with. If our church building falls down, praise God, we'll meet at the park or the beach. We could end up worshiping in jails if we have to someday, due to persecution.

Stop being divided from your brothers and sisters today. God doesn't recognize division in the church. He sees only one Body of Christ, not many. Think about it. If you see many bodies of Christ, what does that tell you?

Christians Still Suffer and
16   **Die for Their Faith**

*Remember the word that I said to you, "A slave is not
greater than his master." If they persecuted Me, they
will also persecute you.*

—JOHN 15:20 NASB

Sometimes we take our freedom in America for granted. The
words we openly speak can cost someone their life in other countries where Christians are martyred for their faith. How often do
we think about our brothers and sisters who are suffering on the
other side of the earth? How often do we remember to pray for
them or to send money to ministries that support the persecuted
church?

In some countries the Christians have to break the ice in the
lake to baptize new believers. In the middle of a cold winter's
night when they won't be seen, they awake and head for the river.
There they chip away a place to immerse those few who have
gathered to be identified with the Lord through baptism. These
folks go under the water a sinner and come up a saved ice cube.

And guess who these persecuted Christians are praying for?
They're praying for us! They're asking God to pour out His Spirit
on us and bless us. And many of these prayers are uttered from
jail cells filled with Baptists, Catholics, Episcopalians, Lutherans,
Presbyterians, Methodists, and Pentecostals. They pray for us,
and they fellowship in the kind of unity that only seems to come
through persecution.

If one of these Christians came to America where they could
freely preach the gospel, they'd probably be jailed here for
disturbing the peace. They're so zealous for the Lord, and I
admire them. They're heroes.

There's a story about an American Christian who was riding a bus in one of these countries. He asked one of his fellow passengers, "Do you know that Jesus loves you?" The other man responded, "Do you know how much trouble you can get in for saying that?" The American looked at him, smiling with tears in his eyes, and answered, "Do you know how much trouble I can get in for *not* saying that?"

In some countries the Christians think the Great Tribulation has already begun. More believers have lost their lives in the past century than in the previous 1,900 years combined. These people are dying because they believe what you believe. They can go to jail for three years just for possessing a Bible—if they could buy one. A Bible sells, underground of course, for one month's salary. Some believers read from Bibles that are hand-copied pages from someone else's Bible. Some churches have only one Bible, which they portion out to members for one hour a week—not to read, but to hand copy.

Meanwhile back in the United States, we fellowship around a pizza and make plans for next week's ball game or beach party. And there's nothing wrong with pizza or ball games or the beach, it's just that the Lord also wants us harvesting souls. He wants us to have a heart for His beaten body around the world. What we do for them, we do for Jesus Himself. To the extent we ignore them, we're ignoring Jesus Himself.

Rejoice always; pray without ceasing; in everything give thanks; for this is God's will for you in Christ Jesus.

—1 THESSALONIANS 5:16-18 NASB

Prayer is the only power a Christian has against Satan. So how come we don't pray more? Satan knows he can't take Jesus away from us—he can't snatch us out of Jesus' hand—but he knows what he *can* do. He knows he can short-circuit our witness to others, he can rob us of our power for living, and he can discourage us by whispering the lies to us that undermine our prayer life. You know what I mean. Satan will say, "Sure, you should pray. But not right now. You're too busy. God will understand." Sometimes we can even get so focused on our work for God that we procrastinate praying. But a prayerless work for God will be an ineffective work for God. And a prayerless *life* will be an ineffective life for God.

Satan might be even bolder by suggesting, "Your prayers don't accomplish anything, so why bother?" He can mount a direct assault on the integrity of God to hear and answer our prayers. He'll do anything to keep us from employing this one mighty weapon God issued to every believer as our own personal atomic bomb against the enemy.

When we find our effectiveness in God's service ebbing or when our personal life is undergoing assault, we should first ask ourselves, "Is my prayer life solid?" Many of the problems we stew over without coming to a resolution could be easily ended by what the believers of an earlier generation called "praying through." Stay on your knees until God gives the witness that the matter is settled. Don't get up a minute too soon.

*You have not received a spirit of slavery leading to fear
again, but you have received a spirit of adoption as
sons by which we cry out, "Abba! Father!"*
—ROMANS 8:15 NASB

Do you remember how it was when you first met Jesus? Do
you remember how you delighted to call God your "Daddy,"
your "Abba, Father"? You enjoyed the intimacy of a child with
its papa. And now how is it? Is He still "Daddy" or has He
become "Reverend Holy Heavenly Father"? Has the intimacy
been replaced with a formalism that keeps Him at arm's
length?

Every Christian, of course, grows out of infancy. We need to
get quickly past the diaper stage and move on into maturity. But
make sure that the maturity is born out of that childlike faith in
our Daddy. Don't let religion rob you of relationship. Jesus didn't
come to start a new religion. There were enough of them already.
He came here to show us the Father and to demonstrate the
depth of His love for sinners.

Before Christ, the veil in the temple separated man from
God. Moses was one of the few people that had some kind of
relationship with God. Appearing in God's presence gave Moses
such radiance that he had to wear a sack over his head so nobody
would see the glow.

But in Jesus, things changed. The curtain in the temple was
torn from top to bottom. We have the access to our Father that
no one else can have. We can come to God's throne as spotless,
redeemed creatures with the perfection of Jesus inside us. In the
flesh, we are still sinful. But in Him, we have become the righteousness of God. Because of Jesus, we're as close to God as a

person can get. And the relationship we enjoy is that of a child with a strong, loving father.

Grow in Christ, but never lose the childlike spirit that cries out boldly, "Abba, Father."

His eyes were like a flame of fire....In His right hand
He held seven stars, and out of His mouth came a
sharp two-edged sword; and His face was like the sun
shining in its strength.

—REVELATION 1:14-16 NASB

Who is Jesus? Many of us were brought up with the image we
see on Christmas cards—the baby in the manger, or on stained
glass windows—the guy on the cross. We have this image of Jesus
as a weakling who got beat up by the bad guys. And yes, Jesus was
ridiculed and scorned by Roman politicians and religious
hypocrites. He did humble Himself to the point of death. And in
our minds, He stays that way.

But Jesus grew up. He's no longer in the manger. And Jesus
was resurrected after His crucifixion; He's been off that cross for
2,000 years. So when you think about Jesus, take Him down off
the cross for a while and think about Him as He will be when He
returns. That's the Jesus we should be looking for.

In the book of Revelation we read the only physical description of the resurrected Jesus given in the Bible. His eyes are like
a flame of fire. His face shines like the sun at noon. In His mouth
is a two-edged sword. That's the Jesus we'll see when we meet
Him face to face. A powerful Jesus. A mighty Jesus. King of Kings
and Lord of Lords! That's the Jesus who is my Jesus. He's the one
who is my best friend, my Redeemer, my elder brother.

And the heaven that you and I are invited to share with this
great Jesus isn't the papier-mâché place where we sit in white
robes endlessly plucking our harps. Instead, Paul tells us that no
eye has seen, nor ear heard, nor thought imagined the wonderful
things that God has waiting for us.

Every day we should look for Jesus' return with great expectation. We have a solid hope in Him. We have a future that is so good, the Bible says don't even try to imagine it—you can't do it. And it's all because we are loved by the mighty God of the universe. All because of His Son who has prepared a place for us.

No, it's not the Jesus of the picture postcard or the stained glass window that we worship; it's the Jesus who is returning as a conquering king.

Even so, come, Lord Jesus!

Even to your old age I will be the same, and even to
your graying years I will bear you!

—ISAIAH 46:4 NASB

Sometimes we think God has forgotten about us. The years pass by and nothing seems to change. God hasn't used us in the way we wanted to be used. Maybe we're still single and wondering why God hasn't let us meet our mate yet and start a family. Or we have the same job we had years ago and there doesn't seem to be much future for the Lord in it.

Moses had to wait. He was 80 years old and in retirement at Israeli Acres before God was ready to use him. And in the years that followed, Moses was used more by God than he had been in his youth and middle age combined.

Noah had to wait. All his neighbors thought he was a crazy man. Here's this 500-year-old guy out back working on a three-story something-or-other. They weren't quite sure what it was. They saw him building a lot of stalls in this monstrous edifice. A hotel maybe? And then the rain began to fall. The laughing-stock of the neighborhood became very popular all of a sudden. But it was too late. God closed the door. Noah was used at the very last minute for something so spectacular in the plan of God that he never could have imagined it as a young man.

Gideon had to wait. He was prepared to face the enemy with a massive army. But God said, "Wait. You've got too many men." And so Gideon waited, listened, and watched while God took away his natural strength until the army stood at only 300; too small to win a battle in the natural, but plenty of power when God's in control.

Corrie ten Boom had to wait. She suffered through Hitler's death camp when she was young, not even sure she would make it out alive. Then in her 40s God began to really work with her. She kept going for the Lord well into her 80s with a divine energy that would put most of us to shame.

Every true servant of God must wait. And then, when you finally think that it's all over for you and that God has passed you over, then He decides to use you. You finally have been stripped of your own hopes, dreams, and strength and must depend on Him. He alone gets the glory. It's God's delight to use people that the world considers useless. He delights to use us when we consider ourselves useless.

Give God time and give God room to work. And wait expectantly.

The Good News

God demonstrates His own love toward us, in that
while we were yet sinners, Christ died for us.
—ROMANS 5:8 NASB

When I was a new believer I thought that if I tried hard enough eventually I'd stop sinning. But what I discovered about myself—and I think you probably have also—is that there's no such thing in this life as sinless perfection. We all stumble in many ways. But even though we can't be *faultless* in this life, we certainly can be *blameless*. Our flesh is full of faults, but praise God, our flesh has been crucified with God and we stand blameless before our heavenly Father. Even more, He's given us His Spirit within us to walk in such a way that we don't have to fulfill the selfish desires of the flesh.

If we're resting in Jesus and full of the Holy Spirit, we can walk with assurance that even when we stumble, we remain forgiven in God's sight. A lot of our behavioral problems are Adam's fault. We inherited our sin nature from him. But Jesus was the "second Adam" and in Him we inherit a new nature that allows us to overcome sin.

Some of our stumbling is the result of Satan's attack on us. But the Holy Spirit in us is greater than "he that is in the world"—Satan.

I've never walked a faultless day in my life. But since I became a Christian, I've never had a day in which the blame for my sin was imputed to me. For I, like you, have a sin-bearer who bore all my sins so that I wouldn't have to.

If you're a Christian, rejoice today. For no matter how fault-filled your day is, you stand blameless in Christ. That's the gospel—that's the good news.

*All the people saw him walking and praising God; and
they were taking note of him as being the one who used
to sit at the Beautiful Gate of the temple to beg alms,
and they were filled with wonder and amazement at
what had happened to him.*

—ACTS 3:9,10 NASB

Peter and John went to the temple one day and they found a
beggar there, lame from his mother's womb. And he stretched
forth his hand toward Peter to receive alms. Peter looked into his
pocket, came up empty, and said, "Hey man, I'm broke. But I'm
not broke spiritually, so what I have, I give to you freely. In the
name of Jesus Christ of Nazareth, get up and walk!"

Medical experts say that when someone's lame all their life, it
takes them about six months to learn how to walk like a toddler.
This guy, though, wasn't up on the medical research, so he got up
and started dancing around, to the dismay of all the Baptists in
the area.

"Don't get so excited about the Lord," everyone told him.
"You're turning into a *fanatic!*" Boy, the devil loves that word.
But let me tell you that when God heals a person, they do get
fanatical. This guy was dancing around and the Temple Baptists
said, "Hey man, stop that dancing." He replied, "Yeah, but David
danced—and so am I!" Not to be outdone, the Baptists said,
"Yeah, but that was 500 years ago. That's not for today. That
stopped when David died."

Today, some folks say that God healed for the first hundred
years or so and then went on vacation or something. I don't
understand this kind of thinking. It doesn't say anywhere in the
Bible that the Holy Spirit will stop working for a while and then

come back. It doesn't say that Jesus Christ changes, it says He's the same yesterday, today, and *forever*. In Malachi, God says, "I am God. I do not change."

God still does what He did in the early days of the church. He still gives us the Holy Spirit and His gifts, He still heals, and He still guides us. Our God can do anything. If we don't praise Him, He can even turn some pebbles into a band of worshiping Christians to praise Him. Don't limit God. He's still El Shaddai—The Almighty One. Tell Him all your needs—physical, emotional, spiritual, financial, vocational—whatever.

God will provide.

Let God Catch You

*It is God who is at work in you, both to will and to
work for His good pleasure.*

—PHILIPPIANS 2:13 NASB

I'm so glad that God can use people who don't necessarily want
to be used. Take Jonah, for example. God wanted him to go to
preach to Nineveh, but Jonah said, "No way. I'm going on a
Mediterranean cruise." So off he went on his vacation. At first
he was having a pretty good time. But then a storm came up.
Wherever the boat turned, the storm followed. It became pretty
obvious to everyone on board that one of the passengers was to
blame. So they drew lots to find out who it was. Five minutes
later Jonah was tossed overboard.

He was out there treading water and telling God, "I'm *still* not
going to Nineveh." So God sent a huge fish to swallow Jonah
and eventually, from the other side of the whale's tonsils, Jonah
gave up. The fish got a bad case of indigestion and spit Jonah up
on a nearby beach. And when Jonah went to Nineveh and
preached repentance, the people listened and were spared. God
used Jonah in spite of his rebellion.

If God has something for you to do, He'll find a way to make
you an offer you can't refuse.

No, He's not the godfather, He's the *heavenly* Father and He
loves each of us so much that He'll set up some roadblocks to
slow us down as we run away from Him. He'll even send a great
fish to swallow us up until we're ready to get spit out into the
mission He has for us.

I don't know why God is so patient with us; I just know that
He is. I don't know why He loves us, but I know that He does.

John 3:16 doesn't say, "For God so loved the world because…," it just says, "For God so loved the world."

If you're running from God, slow down. Let Him catch you. Skip the step of being swallowed by the fish—it isn't pretty.

Get in God's flow and stay there. That's where rest awaits you.

24   Who Is Writing the Checks?

Consider it pure joy, my brothers, whenever you face
trials of many kinds, because you know that the test-
ing of your faith develops perseverance.

—JAMES 1:2-4

Have you ever wondered why God allows so much trouble to come into our life? For instance, I know that when I'm sick, it's not because God *wants* me sick. But sometimes He allows it to come upon me as a reminder of who's in charge of my life.

The same thing happens with money. I know He doesn't want me to worry and fret over all my bills, but sometimes He allows the money to get short so that I'm reminded that He's my source of supply. I'm in danger when you hear me say, "Hey, I'm doing great! I've got a lot of concerts lined up and my albums are selling well. My bank account is lookin' good and there's smooth sailing ahead."

The next thing I know, I'm asking, "What happened, God? I know I haven't talked to You for a while. Um, where are the checks?"

Then I hear, "Well, son, you seemed to forget that they were coming from Me, so I thought I'd cut them off for a while to remind you."

Ouch.

God wants us healthy, happy, and focused on Him. When we get our eyes off Him and trouble comes, don't greet it as if it were your enemy. Welcome the trials that God sends as messengers to bring you back to Him. When the headaches come, go to the Lord first, not the aspirin bottle. Only worry when the trials stop coming to remind you of your dependence on Him.

25   His Love Came Over Me

*I have been crucified with Christ; and it is no longer I
who live, but Christ lives in me; and the life which I
now live in the flesh I live by faith in the Son of God,
who loved me and gave Himself up for me.*

—GALATIANS 2:20 NASB

When I accepted the Lord into my life I had trouble following
Him, as do many people. When I asked Him into my life I understood that His death on the cross was for my sins, but then in
some ways, I kept living the way I had been before I was saved.
But then the Lord said, "Wait a minute, Keith. I did that for you;
wouldn't you like to do something for Me?"

I answered, "Uh, sure Lord. What do You want from me?"

"Oh, I think I'll take everything," was God's reply.

"Everything?" I asked.

"Every last bit of it. I want it all," God answered.

"Wait, God, I'm not sure I understand," I said.

"Oh, I think you do. Keith, I want you to dedicate your *life* to
Me. I want you to give Me your music, your money, your activi-
ties. I want it *all*. I'll tell you how to spend your money; I'll give
you the songs to sing; I'll guide you where I want you to go."

I gulped and said, "Uh, well God, if that's what You want...I
guess there's no turning back now." So I gave God everything I
had in the best way I knew how. I'm sure I made mistakes, but
I was a baby Christian muddling along like new babies do.

The thing was, the more I tried to give God everything, the
harder it was. Then one day I ran into the Holy Spirit. He knew
how hard I had been trying and how often I'd failed and He said,
"Keith, you're striving to do something that you can't do in your

own strength. Why don't you let Me do it for you? You get in the backseat, and I'll do the driving. I'll do the giving up."

I said, "This can't be God; this is too easy. I've been trying so hard and I'm so proud of myself—nah, I better keep working at my Christianity."

The Holy Spirit gently pressed on. "Keith, don't try so hard. Just let Me take over, and I'll do all I've planned to do *through* you."

That was a revelation for me. I had it in my mind that when you became a Christian, God kind of put you in shackles and chains against the wall. I didn't know about God providing rest. I had no idea that Christianity was so simple. I gave in to Him and allowed Him to live through me. I still made plenty of mistakes and often fell back into trying to please God in my own strength, but when I did, He was faithful to remind me that I had gotten back in the driver's seat, and would I please return to the backseat?

Every believer must have that day when they meet the Holy Spirit and hear His offer to take over the responsibility for living the Christian life. That day came for me. Has it come for you?

Be of sober spirit, be on the alert. Your adversary, the devil, prowls around like a roaring lion, seeking someone to devour.

—1 PETER 5:8 NASB

I had been a Christian for a while when I began to notice a sort of boredom setting in. I was getting tired of going to Bible studies, tired of praying, tired of a lot of what had become simply routine in my life.

That boredom was like an alarm going off. I knew that it signaled a love for the Lord that was cooling off, and I knew I didn't want that to happen. I remembered that in the book of Revelation Jesus had rebuked the Laodiceans for leaving their first love. I was determined I would never be guilty of being a Laodicean. So what was happening to me? Why was I growing cold?

Then I realized that one of Satan's strategies is to try and take God's covenant with us, which is eternally new and fresh, and turn it into something old, cold, and stale. He whispers to us that our Christianity is just "religion" and that it's old and boring. Pretty soon, we yawn and agree, "Yeah, this *is* pretty boring." If we accept those thoughts injected by Satan, our faith *will* become old and boring.

We have to constantly be on guard of our thought life. We need to develop the ability to discern the difference between God's voice, Satan's voice, and our own thoughts. And when we know that what's being whispered in our ear is a lie from the enemy, we need to be quick to tell Satan to get lost.

If you saw a dog digging through your garbage, would you sit there watching and think, *You know, I really want that dog to quit messing with my garbage*—or would you start yelling at the dog and chasing him off? In the same way, we need to get after Satan, that dirty dog, when he starts digging up garbage and spreading it around in our minds. The mind is where the battle is won or lost. We need to be diligent in keeping guard over the thoughts we accept as truth. A lie from Satan, if accepted as truth, will result in eventual deception. Be watchful over your thought life.

...though now for a little while you may have had to suffer grief in all kinds of trials. These have come so that your faith—of greater worth than gold, which perishes even though refined by fire—may be proved genuine and may result in praise.

—1 PETER 1:6,7

Every Christian should be yearning for a deeper walk with the Lord than what he or she has. Maturity is a never-ending process because we never can reach perfection in this life. We'll always be making mistakes or misunderstanding our circumstances to some degree, but as we grow those times should be less and less.

And as much as we all like to get the goosebump feelings that signal an emotional high, it's not then that we really grow any deeper in the Lord. Instead God chooses to use trials to deepen our faith and to conform us to the image of Christ. Sure, we go "ouch" or "that hurts!" but God is using those trials to sand us like a fine diamond. The problem is that most of us run from the trials God sends us. We don't want to grow if there's a bit of pain involved. But if we open our arms, embrace the trial God sends—give it a big hug, it will disappear as a trial and return as a blessing. If you love your trial, it isn't a trial anymore. If you can say, "Thank You, Lord. I don't want to be any other place but where I am right now, because I know this is the place where You want me," then that place becomes God's *safe* place for you.

That attitude removes the trouble from the trial. The way to victory over a trial isn't to run away from it, which is our natural inclination, but to *love* it. The same is true with a person. We all have someone in our life who is obnoxious or maybe just a trial to us. Our natural response is to stay away from such a person until God answers our prayer to "change him, God, change him!" Instead, let your prayer become, "God, *don't* change him until You're through using him the way he is in my life. I want to learn how to love him the way he is." When you pray that way, and mean it, that person is no longer a trial to you.

Today is the day for you to embrace your trial, whether it's circumstances or another person. Turn the trial into blessing and watch God move.

*Where can I go from your Spirit? Where can I flee
from your presence? If I go up to the heavens, you are
there; if I make my bed in the depths, you are there. If
I rise on the wings of the dawn, if I settle on the far side
of the sea, even there your hand will guide me, your
right hand will hold me fast.*

—PSALM 139:7-10

God is so good. He's so patient with us. He's so forgiving. I don't
believe that anyone is going to hell until they've had a chance to
meet Him. If they respond to Jesus, they'll be saved. There's
nothing you or I have done that's so bad as to keep us out of
heaven, once we've repented of it. And there's no time limit—
except the day we die or when Jesus returns. Many people say,
"Religion is for old people, so when I get old I'll become a
Christian." The problem is that many people never get old. They
spend their youth on their own lusts and desires with no thought
that God sees and records all our deeds. And while they're living
like this, they die unsaved, still in their youth, their hope gone
forever.

But as Christians, as believers, as born-again Spirit-filled
lovers of Jesus Christ, there's nothing to worry about. He's blot-
ted out the blackness on our record and turned up the brightness
in our lives, which is Him. This is the grace of God. And there's
a day coming when we will receive a jewel for every moment
we've spent with Him, for each time we've not worked for Him
but have let Him work through us. If we try to work for Him, we
fall on our face in the mud. If we rest and allow Him to work
through us, then we get the grace flowing through us as a glove
has the hand going through it, doing all the good things a hand

can do. And what does a glove have to do to be used? Does it have to sit there all nervous on the dresser trying to wait for the hand—"C'mon hand. Let's go, hand." No way. It just waits there and the hand comes and fills it up. But can you imagine if the glove only let the hand come in halfway? And the fingers of the glove are dangling from the end of the glove? How effective can the glove or the hand be if it's only half available?

The hand of God looks today for empty gloves He can touch the world with. There have always been only a few who will truly empty themselves to be used by God without reservation. In each new generation God watches to see who will be the ones He can use to continue His work on earth. It's never too soon and it's never too late to say to God, "Here am I, Lord. Use *me*."

29   Jesus Loves to Be with Us

*The LORD longs to be gracious to you; he rises to show
you compassion.*

—ISAIAH 30:18

Many Christians never fully understand just how much God
wants to be their friend. How *intimately* He wants to know them.
Because they've experienced some rejection from others in the
past, they can't fully believe that God won't find some reason to
reject them. If they only understood that God doesn't reject
those who come to Him—He *welcomes* them. He longs to fill
every nook and cranny of the lives of His people with Himself,
but they hold back, unsure of full surrender.

Like most Christians, I didn't give myself totally to God all at
once. I asked Him into my life and went on doing what I thought
I was supposed to be doing. I read the Bible, I witnessed, I
prayed—all that stuff. But then one day God said, "I want more."
There was this knock on the door of the secret closet which I had
held apart from God, to be alone with myself. Where He couldn't
come in or hear or see what I was doing—or so I imagined.

But when God knocked on the door of the closet, it was with
these words that pierced my heart, "Keith, I want to be where
you are. Can I come in?"

God wanted to be where I was? He wanted to be with *me*?
Then I realized He didn't care so much about my possessions, or
my music, or my ministry, or anything else. He didn't die for any
of those *things*. He died for *me*. And now He wanted to be where
I was. I knew then that I really had no place to hide—and that I
didn't *want* to hide anymore from such a friend.

Don't wait any longer to let Him into that secret closet. He
wants to be where *you* are.

*If you have any encouragement from being united with
Christ, if any comfort from his love, if any fellowship
with the Spirit, if any tenderness and compassion, then
make my joy complete by being like-minded.*

— PHILIPPIANS 2:2

Are you excited about Jesus? Can other people see the joy of the Lord in your face? I've noticed that too few Christians radiate the presence of the Lord in their life. They look like they were baptized in vinegar! They seem to have this image of Christianity that requires them to have a grim, gray look on their face. It's like they're saying, "Well, praise God, it's such a *burden* to be a Christian. All the Bibles I have to carry around. Why is this darn concordance so big and heavy? Well, I guess I have to take some time out and *praaayyyy* now. Sigh."

What kind of testimony is that?! If you're happy (and if you're a redeemed child of God you certainly *ought* to be happy), then you better show it on your face. That's what the world is looking to see in the life of the Christian. The world is tired of seeing hypocrites. If it weren't for *religion* I would have become a Christian two years earlier than I did.

What I saw as an unbeliever seeking the truth was a bunch of guys running around with their religious theories and pet doctrines, instead of proclaiming by their words and actions the truth of Jesus Christ. I saw them all sticking together in what seemed like little cliques, instead of reaching out.

As a result, I didn't become a Christian through going to a church service. I *couldn't* have become a Christian, because I wouldn't have been caught dead in a church. All the churches I'd seen had been full of hypocrites. Sure, I was wrong—I was a judger of men—but that's the way unbelievers act. I wanted to know if these supposed "ambassadors for Jesus" really could *show* me Jesus Christ by the way they lived. I never found one. Looking back, I'm sure there *were* some—not all Christians are as joyless as the ones I met—but I didn't run across any who had anything to offer that I wanted.

Rest assured there are a lot of searchers out there, just like I was. They may not tell you they're looking for God, but they are. And when they look at your life, do they see Him?

*Be on the alert, for you do not know which day your
Lord is coming.*

—MATTHEW 24:42 NASB

Summer Snow

Unexpectedly, You came back to see,
If I'd been waiting,
Like I promised long before.
Your shadow filled the room,
The music changed its tune,
When I saw You, You were standing at the door.

Like summer snow, You were an unexpected sight.
A blazing sun, You were shining in the night,
When I really should have known
That You'd be coming home.

I waited patiently, but I found it hard to see,
If You were coming,
Why was there such a long delay?
At times I thought You lied,
Or else You would have tried,
To let me know that You were coming home today.

Like summer snow, it falls around me in the cold.
I can hear the echoes of the warnings I was told.
That I should know,
That You'd be coming home.

Like summer snow, You were an unexpected sight.
A blazing sun, You were shining in the night,
When I really should have known,
That You'd be coming home.
Unexpectedly, You came back to see.

I wrote "Summer Snow" with Melody for Christians who walked up the church aisle to accept Christ, but they never really turned their lives over to Him. They thought to themselves, *Well, I said the prayer, now I'll go back to doing what I was doing.* These are people who professed to love the light, but yet they continue to walk in darkness.

If you're a Christian, then the light of God lives in you and the darkness around you is evident and it repels you. But if you think darkness is light, then there's something very wrong. I've run into a lot of these people. Sometimes they're called "carnal Christians"; sometimes they're referred to as "backsliders." I call them "Christians in Big Trouble." I'm not judging them as to their eternal destination, but even if they stay saved, they're headed for big trouble in *this* life. Satan is a stern taskmaster. He will subtly rope you, maybe even masquerading as an angel of light, but his goal for you is destruction. Darkness always leads to destruction.

If you're a Christian, then you've been called *out* of darkness into a new kingdom entirely. What foolishness to have the light and yet remain in the darkness under the spell of your mortal enemy, the prince of darkness.

If you love Jesus, *follow Him*. Get out of the darkness. Have no portion with any of the works of the enemy. If you flirt with darkness long enough, you'll be sucked into a world of trouble, heartache, and despair in the darkness.

What are the dark places that Satan has invited you to visit? What has he promised? A sensual thrill? Friends? Popularity? Money? Rest assured that he has some special offer that he's designed specifically for your weaknesses. Don't be ignorant of his devices. Humble yourself before God, turn away from the darkness, and the enemy will flee.

If I preach the gospel, I have nothing to boast of, for I am under compulsion; for woe is me if I do not preach the gospel.

—1 CORINTHIANS 9:16 NASB

Who is the Jesus we follow? Today, the Jesus most people hear about is the bumper sticker Jesus, the Jesus who makes money for us when we put Him on our products. The toothbrush Jesus, the T-shirt Jesus—the one we can market and make money from—the Jesus that's out there for public consumption.

But the real Jesus isn't very commercial. The real Jesus wasn't too popular with a lot of people. In some cities they asked Him to leave. That's what'll happen if you follow this Jesus Christ. Paul the apostle wasn't too popular either. He wasn't invited back to many cities either—but he went anyway. He had to proclaim the news that Jesus was the Messiah, come to save sinners from their sins. All of the disciples, except for John, died horrible deaths for their faith. Even John underwent imprisonment and torture. Do you think this was because their message was so popular? No, it was because these men were sold out for Jesus. They weren't once-a-week Christians or even twice-a-week Christians. They weren't even seven-times-a-week Christians. They were on duty as Christians *all the time.* They might have gotten by if they'd just softened their message a little—if they'd just made Jesus a little more popular.

Too bad they couldn't take a lesson from us and offer up our compromised Jesus, the commercial Jesus who looks attractive in all the paintings—a real movie-star quality about Him. And yet in Isaiah we read about the real Jesus:

> *He had no beauty or majesty to attract us to him,*
> *nothing in his appearance that we should desire him.*
> *He was despised and rejected by men,*
> *a man of sorrows, and familiar with suffering.*
> *Like one from whom men hide their faces*
> *he was despised, and we esteemed him not.*
>
> —ISAIAH 53:2,3

Is this the Jesus we see today? Usually not. Instead it's the Jesus of the shag haircut, the bronze tan, the trimmed beard, and of course, the FM radio voice.

If you follow this Jesus, you might actually get to retain your standing with the world. But if you follow the Jesus who was crucified, the Jesus who called sinners to repentance, the Jesus who requires denial of self as requirement to follow Him, then you can kiss popularity with the world good-bye. If you're a student, don't expect to be BMOC. If you're a politician, don't expect to be reelected. If you follow this Jesus, you might not even be popular in your church. Sometimes *I'm* not very popular because my message is perceived as too hard. "C'mon Keith," I'll hear. "Don't be so gloomy. Make us laugh. Make us smile. Sing your happy songs for us."

Face it, the truth isn't much in demand. People would prefer a lie that allows them to live their lives in their comfort zones. Of course, it's not as if it's *really* a lie—more like just a minor compromise. God doesn't mind compromise—does He?

But if we compromise the truth, how is it any longer the truth? A little yeast leavens the whole loaf. Today we have the choice of which Jesus we're following. And the choice we make will have an eternal effect.

33 Mercy Triumphs Over Judgment

Speak and act as those who are going to be judged by the law that gives freedom, because judgment without mercy will be shown to anyone who has not been merciful. Mercy triumphs over judgment!

—JAMES 2:12,13

People will disappoint us every time. Humans make mistakes. If my faith relied on the infallibility of my pastor, I'd be a goner. I'm blessed that God has given me a good pastor to lead me into the Word of God and to counsel me. And man, I sure wouldn't want to be a Christian without a pastor. But I know he's a man just like I am.

I know that if I put my faith in any human being, I'll soon be disillusioned and hurt. And guess what? If anybody puts their faith in me, they're *really* in for trouble. I'm so human, it scares me sometimes. We all make so many mistakes—it's like part of our job description as human beings.

I didn't understand this early in my Christian walk. The first time I went to church as a new believer, I sat in the back row and watched. At first I was really amazed—wow, all these believers gathered together to worship the Lord. But then Satan came and took a seat beside me. He leaned over and whispered, "Look at that girl up there with the beehive hairdo. And look at all that makeup! She can't be saved.

"And what about that guy in the front row? He's got his arm around the girl next to him. Doesn't he know this is church and his attention is supposed to be on God?"

After a few minutes Satan directed me to a guy who was leafing through his Bible too roughly and accidentally tore a page.

"That's terrible," Satan said. "What kind of church is this anyway?"

Satan always likes to sit next to new Christians. He's got a lot of advice for them and is eager to show the new believer how to judge others in the body. But after a while, when you've dared to move up a few pews, you turn around and realize that the newest believer is now looking at you, listening to Satan's accusations about *you*. Then you have to admit, "Yep, Satan, you've got it right this time. I'm a man who makes plenty of mistakes and probably offends a lot of people. Why, if it wasn't for God's grace, I'd be in a real mess."

When you really understand God's grace toward you, the vilest offender of all, then you somehow find the grace to give to others in their humanity. Stop judging others. Give them as much grace as you want to receive from God.

Perseverance must finish its work so that you may be
mature and complete, not lacking anything. If any of
you lacks wisdom, he should ask God, who gives
generously to all without finding fault, and it will be
given to him.

—JAMES 1:4,5

When I first came to the Lord I was leading people to Jesus all the time. And then I turned around and stepped on their toes. I was so zealous. I pulled them into the kingdom and then I stomped on them.

My pastor didn't know what to do with me. He called *his* pastor, Chuck Smith, and said, "I don't know what to do with this guy Keith Green. He's leading people to the Lord like flies to honey, and then they're getting all offended by him."

Chuck's answer to my pastor, as he later reported it to me, changed my whole walk with the Lord. I suppose someone might think Chuck counseled my pastor to urge me to slow down a bit or to cool it. But what he said was, "It's better to be overzealous for the Lord than lukewarm. Leave him alone. He'll grow." And I did.

As I grew in the Lord, I began to understand a lot more about grace and about forgiveness and eventually that found its way into my life and my ministry. But God did it. It wasn't the result of listening to a man tell me to simmer down a bit. Zeal for the Lord is good. Go out and take a chance. If you try to do ten things for the Lord and you make three mistakes, then you've at least done seven things right. But if you're afraid to make those three mistakes, you won't do anything. Do the ten things God gives you. Take the chance that three or even five or more might be wrong. God will forgive you.

Make sure, though, that what you're doing is scriptural. Don't do what you know is wrong and cover your sin by calling it "zeal for the Lord." If you'll just move out for God, He'll bless you and you'll see your mistakes, learn from them, and pretty soon, you're making fewer mistakes and God is using you to build His kingdom.

35   Staying Where God Has You

You are the light of the world. A city on a hill cannot be hidden. Neither do people light a lamp and put it under a bowl. Instead they put it on its stand, and it gives light to everyone in the house. In the same way, let your light shine before men, that they may see your good deeds and praise your Father in heaven.

—MATTHEW 5:14-16

God loves radical faith. Lukewarmness, however, makes God sick. Paul was a radical Christian. He went where he wasn't invited, and he spoke the message God gave him unashamedly. He was fanatical about his love for God to the point of not caring about what people thought of him. He was bound to preach, come heaven or high water. By his actions Paul left us an example. He tells us to "be imitators of me as I am of Christ."

When I became a Christian I was working as a songwriter for CBS Publishing. I asked the Lord if I should give up that job, now that I was a believer. I was ready to go wherever God wanted me. But He wanted me where I was. He told me to stay put. Later I would see the wisdom in that decision as I was able to witness to those around me at CBS. These guys saw me turn from a young, money-mongering, self-centered guy who wanted a hit song at any cost to a Christian man who wanted to see the Lord glorified above all else.

These guys couldn't figure me out. I started saying "God bless you" to them when I left for the day. They'd turn to one another with puzzled expressions like, "I didn't sneeze, did you?" For some time they thought I was crazy or got some bad drugs or something. But more and more, I'd sit down and talk with them about their problems and offer to pray for them. They began to see that the changes that were going on in my life were real and they were *good*.

Then one day the president of CBS called me. He said, "Keith, there's this one Christian song that you wrote that if you'd just change a couple of the lyrics, Olivia Newton-John will record it and it will be a surefire hit. It's a guaranteed $100,000 to $200,000 the first year and an average of $25,000 to $50,000 for the next few years after that."

But I knew that song was God's song. I didn't even blink an eye—God gave me the boldness and the grace to say, "That song isn't mine. I don't have the right to change the lyrics." They understood what I was saying, but they couldn't believe it. But after that, they never made fun of my faith again.

Then later the whole CBS staff got fired, except for the writers. These guys would call me up every once in a while, and I'd tell them I was praying for them, and they'd thank me and tell me that they really needed my prayers. I stayed where God wanted me and the result was blessing. Later He would call me to leave, but it was in His time, not mine.

Staying or leaving is God's call, not ours. But whichever He chooses, we must obey it. When you let your light shine in dark places, the result is great blessing—first to you, then to those around you, and also to the Lord Himself.

If anyone is ashamed of me and my words, the Son of Man will be ashamed of him when he comes in his glory and in the glory of the Father.

—LUKE 9:26

There's a story about a little boy who got saved at church one Sunday. The next day he was scheduled to leave for summer camp, and he was worried about what all the other little kids would say if they knew he had become a Christian.

His mother told him, "Just shine your light, follow the Lord, and everything will be fine." So off he went to camp.

A week later he returned home, and his mom asked how it went.

"It was great," the boy replied. "They didn't suspect a thing."

That's the attitude of a lot of Christians—to try and live our lives in such a way that our non-Christian friends or our co-workers or fellow students don't "suspect a thing" about our faith.

What are we afraid of? Rejection? If they reject us for our faith, then great is our reward in heaven. And when they reject us, our heavenly Father receives us.

Think about it. Whose opinion do you value most, that of your friends—or the God who loved you so much He gave the best in heaven to redeem you?

Suppose a man comes into your meeting wearing a gold ring and fine clothes, and a poor man in shabby clothes also comes in. If you show special attention to the man wearing fine clothes and say, "Here's a good seat for you," but say to the poor man, "You stand there" or "Sit on the floor by my feet," have you not discriminated among yourselves and become judges with evil thoughts?

—JAMES 2:2-4

You can't please everybody. Sometimes my music is too straight for hippies, and sometimes it's too weird for straight people. And God loves them all—hippie and straight. We need to be careful about how we judge others and what we insist on when they hear the gospel. You know you wouldn't go to Mexico and make everyone learn English in order to hear the gospel. No, you preach the good news to them in the language they understand. Musically, don't make all your young people become old people to hear the gospel. Let them hear the gospel in the language they understand.

John Michael Talbot is a good friend of mine. When he came to the Lord, he had very long hair, down past the middle of his back. He walked up the church aisle broken before the Lord. The tears were streaming down his face onto his long beard. A bit later, he returned to his seat and everyone was thinking, *Praise God, the hippie got saved.* And then the usher came up to him and whispered, "Now, son...about that hair."

Seriously! That's like if a black man came up the aisle and the usher said, "Now, son, about your color..." or if a poor person came to a rich church and was told, " Now, son, about that jalopy you drive..."

We can't put people in classes! We can't tolerate a first-, second-, or third-class citizenship in heaven. What is a Christian anyway? Is it how you look, how you speak, how much money you make, what kind of car you drive, how pretty you are?

The only test of a Christian is "Who do you know?" You gotta know people in high places to be a Christian. So if someone says to you, "I'm a Christian," and you doubt it, ask them, "Who do you know?" Don't bother with what they look like or smell like. After all, Jesus was probably a pretty sweaty guy. His beard was probably a little stringy after tramping around the dusty roads of Israel. If Jesus sat in your church, you might not want to be sitting next to Him. But for the women who loved Him, all they could think to do was to wash His feet with their tears.

Recently the Lord showed me something very important. He said, "Pick out the person you like least in your church…That's how much you love Me, Keith."

I answered, "But Lord, he's so obnoxious. You're not that way."

Jesus responded, "I died for him. I shed my blood for *him*. His obnoxiousness will burn up when he goes through the fire. You're supposed to love him as you love Me."

So go ahead, think about it. Who is it in your church: the guy with the religious affectation in his voice who moans "Halle-luuuuuujahhhhh" during his long, drawn-out prayers, the lady who reeks of cheap perfume, the kid who chomps away on his gum during the service? Think about that person—or those people—and start to see them through the eyes of Jesus. Love them as you love Him. Sure it's hard. But for someone else in your church, maybe you're the person they're thinking about right now. You're the one they have a hard time loving. Give the most grace to the least lovable, and you'll experience the grace God has reserved for you.

38   Let Jesus Clean You Up

"Come now, let us reason together," says the LORD. "Though your sins are like scarlet, they shall be as white as snow; though they are red as crimson, they shall be like wool."

—ISAIAH 1:18

God takes us as we are. Heaven is a "come-as-you-are" invitation. I've met backslidden Christians who say, "I'll come back to the Lord someday, but I've got some sins to erase and some problems to work out first." That's like saying you need to clean yourself up before you take a bath.

I always urge backsliders to let the Lord handle their problems. All they need to do is enter into His forgiveness for their sins. If they wait until they make things right themselves, they'll never come back.

We forget that Jesus came to save *sinners*, not the righteous. He loved the woman taken in adultery at the very time the legalistic Pharisees were ready to stone her for her sins. God loves failures. In fact He loves to *use* failures. Moses wasn't eloquent of speech—some theologians think he may have stuttered—yet God used him. He uses me—and if you ask a lot of people, they'll tell you how much better a choice He could have made to win others to Christ.

If you've backslidden, or if you've become paralyzed by your failures, or if you have a sense that God can't use someone with your lack of talent, think again. God searches the earth for those whose hearts are humbled by their lack of ability. These are the very ones God will use.

A thousand may fall at your side, ten thousand at your
right hand, but it will not come near you.

—PSALM 91:7

As Christians living in the end times, we can't expect God to protect us from the suffering caused by other men. In fact, we're told we will suffer persecution for our faith. However, we're also assured that as God pours out His wrath on the earth, He will spare the church.

One way He can spare us is to take us out of the earth during judgment—that's what He did with Lot. Or, as with Noah, He can float us on top of the trouble around us. In Goshen, the children of Israel were smack-dab in the middle of all the plagues, and God put a sort of covering over the land and none of the plagues hit Goshen, which of course made the Egyptians very mad. Although it was dark in all of Egypt, there was a light over Goshen. The land was protected from the judgment of God.

God wants to protect His people, and today His people are the church. He has a shield over the church to protect her from the wiles of the world. The church is the Bride of Christ, and He won't allow His bride to be ravished by the devil.

As part of His church, you can be safe from judgment and the strategies of the enemy. Draw close to God; live under His shield of protection. There is no safer place to be. It's a place of rest.

Hearing that Jesus had silenced the Sadducees, the Pharisees got together. One of them, an expert in the law, tested him with this question: "Teacher, which is the greatest commandment in the Law?"

Jesus replied: " 'Love the Lord your God with all your heart and with all your soul and with all your mind.' This is the first and greatest commandment. And the second is like it: 'Love your neighbor as yourself.' All the Law and the Prophets hang on these two commandments."

—MATTHEW 22:34-40

God requires two things from us from which everything else we do flows. He wants us to love Him first, and He wants us to love one another. And if we do the latter, it'll be proof that we're doing the former. From these two commandments all of the law is fulfilled. These two commandments are inseparable. It's impossible for me to love my brother without the Holy Spirit of God loving through me because, to tell you the truth, I'm pretty selfish—and so are you.

If I don't love my brothers, God says this is proof that I don't love Him either. If I love others, then I'm showing that I love Jesus. Love is the most basic application of our faith. If we don't love, we don't know the One who *is* love.

We've all heard the expression "a face only a mother could love." That's because mothers naturally love their babies. It's in their nature as mothers to love. If they don't love their children, then there's something terribly wrong. And if Christians don't love, then there's something majorly wrong with their faith. But when they do love, their faith moves mountains.

When There's Love

Take some time, make a friend of a stranger,
Touch a hand, just reach out, there's no danger.
When there's love mountains move,
The blind can see and things improve.
Don't be afraid to take the lead,
And be the first to plant a seed,
And then just watch it grow, don't you know?

Take some time, tell someone that you love them,
Make them feel there's a rainbow above them.
When there's love, storms will cease,
And those in chains will be released.
There's not a thing that love can't do,
But it's got to start with me and you,
And then just watch it grow, don't you know?

When there's love, you can't lose,
You'll always know which road to choose,
There's not one thing that love can't do,
But it's got to start with me and you.
And then just watch it grow, don't you know?

Take some time, make a friend of a stranger,
When there's love touch a hand,
Just reach out, there's no danger.
When there's love, take some time,
Make a friend of a stranger.
When there's love!

41　　The Cure for Spiritual Cancer

He said to them, "Go into all the world and preach the good news to all creation."

—MARK 16:15

Far too many Christians remain fence-sitters all their life. But God calls us off the fence into the fields to work for a harvest. Everyone has something to which God has called them. It may take a while to figure out what it is, but if you just start moving, God will give you the direction to go.

Fence-sitters, or lukewarmies, hate it when their friends get off the fence and get hot for God. They feel threatened seeing someone doing what they know they should be doing too. "Hey man, do you have to be such a fanatic?" they ask. "Can't you keep it to yourself?"

No, sorry, we can't. Ain't gonna happen. 'Cause if we're quiet, the rocks will rise up and worship God.

Believe it or not, a *pastor* once said to me, "My relationships with my wife and the Lord are private. I don't go making out with my wife on the street, and I don't go talking about Jesus either. It's private."

I guess this guy figures that when Jesus said to put your light up on the lampstand for all to see, that He was calling for privacy. And when Jesus said a city on a hill can't be hidden, He was calling for privacy. And when He told us to go and preach the good news, it was really a call to privacy. I suppose we've just mistranslated it or something.

I bet this same pastor, if he found a cure for cancer, wouldn't be so "private" about it. If he had any compassion at all, he'd try to get that cure to as many cancer patients as he could. And yet we have a cure for something much worse than cancer of the body, we have a cure for cancer of the *spirit*. This spiritual cancer is called sin, and it's an epidemic that leaves no one untouched and is always terminal unless the cure we have been given—the blood of Jesus—is offered to others.

Folks, Jesus is tired of lukewarmies. He's tired of fence-sitters and pew-warmers. He's looking for on-fire men and women who not only say what they mean, but *do* what they mean.

It's time—no, it's past time—to start doing. We can't do it without the Holy Spirit, of course, but He's there waiting for us. He says, "C'mon. Ask Me, ask Me. I'll help you." God is wanting and waiting to do some good work through *you*.

There is a good work *today* that God has assigned for you to do. Watch for it and do it.

42   Believing Without Seeing

Though you have not seen him, you love him; and
even though you do not see him now, you believe in
him and are filled with an inexpressible and glorious
joy.

—1 Peter 1:8

We fall into trouble when we insist on seeing first, then believing. That's why many people will never see the kingdom of God. We share the gospel and they say, "I don't believe in what I can't see. I can't see God, so I don't believe in Him."

Yet these same skeptics will watch a TV show comprised of invisible waves broadcast through the air. They'll listen to the radio without having to see the radio waves being transmitted to their receiver. They'll warm their dinner in a microwave and believe that invisible microwaves are able to heat their food. And all around them God has created a beautiful earth, and given us brains and bodies that work far more intricately than man-made machinery, and yet "seeing" this creation, they still won't believe.

I was once trying to explain to someone how Jesus doesn't come to your five senses. Our natural senses can lie to us. For instance, there's only a certain spectrum of light that we can see with these little orbs in our sockets. There are only certain sounds we can hear with these funny-looking ears on the side of our head. And yet there is light that we can't see and sounds we can't hear—a dog whistle is an example. We can still believe in these, even without seeing them.

And when we're born again, we receive from God new eyes and new ears and a new heart. They're not *physical*, but they're real nonetheless. Flesh and blood can never enter the kingdom of God. Our earthly body is clueless when it comes to figuring out God. And those who must *see* God before they believe in Him will never be saved.

And those of us who must see victory before we receive it will never be victorious.

*Take up the shield of faith, with which you can extin-
guish all the flaming arrows of the evil one.*

—EPHESIANS 6:16

When you become a Christian, you quickly discover that you
have an enemy. But many believers get so caught up in watching
for the devil that their focus is on him instead of the Lord Jesus.
Be *aware* of his strategies, but don't let your mind dwell on him.

Once you get a good enough glimpse of Satan and you understand his utter vileness and his personal hatred for you, then you
must turn your focus on the victory over him that Jesus won on
the cross. Let the Victor be the object of your attention, not the
defeated enemy.

As believers, we're hidden inside the Lord. Utterly safe and
protected. As long as we abide in Him, we have no fear of the
devil. None. His tricks are no threat to us when we stay hidden
in Christ. As children we used to hide from our enemies and
chant, "Nah, nah, you can't get me!" And that's kind of how we
can react to Satan.

When I was a boy, there was this popular TV program, *Lost in
Space*, about the Robinson family, who was marooned in space.
When they were threatened by approaching meteorites, they
would put up this really cool force field, and the meteorites
would just bounce off. The Robinsons were safe because the force
field protected them. As believers, we're "lost in Jesus." And
when we're abiding in Him, Satan can throw his fiery darts our
way—and rest assured he *will* throw them our way—but they
bounce right off God's force field that protects us.

The Lord is so powerful and Satan is such a jerk. Sometimes I
just don't understand why he just doesn't pack it in and give up.

Maybe it's because the Lord uses him in these last days to separate the sheep from the goats. Maybe it's so we are forced to choose sides as to whom we'll serve.

In Eden God put the Tree of the Knowledge of Good and Evil in the middle of the garden, and Adam and Eve had a choice as to whether to obey or not. Today it's almost like Satan is a tree of good and evil. You can eat of his fruit and be "wise" for a season and gain the approval of the world and maybe some wealth and fame. Satan has these goodies to offer us. He even offered them to Jesus when he said, "See all the kingdoms of the world, all the riches? I'll give you all these if You'll just bow down and worship me." Jesus didn't deny that Satan had the power to offer these temptations. He didn't say, "Satan, you're a liar. It's not in your power to offer Me the world and its riches." His response was, "It is written, worship the Lord thy God and Him only." Basically Jesus was choosing *a torturous death on the cross* rather than the worldly esteem that comes from following Satan.

We all face the same temptation. We can have a measure of success and esteem in this world, or we can reject Satan's offer of temporal comfort and choose the cross. When we choose the cross, we also get the power to ride herd over the enemy, the power to stand behind that force field that repels Satan's stupid temptations and ugly accusations against us.

Never, never forget that as a Christian you walk in Christ's victory over the devil. God's force field protects you from every plan of the enemy. Rejoice then, for it's God's good pleasure to see you walk in victory.

44   Well Done, My Servant

Take My yoke upon you and learn from Me, for I am gentle and humble in heart, and you will find rest for your souls. For My yoke is easy and My burden is light.

—MATTHEW 11:29,30 NASB

God is so good. He alone is worthy of praise. He's the Creator and Sustainer of all things, and totally self-sufficient in His being. And yet, wonder of wonders, He chooses to love us, pursue us, and *use* us.

God doesn't need us. He can use anything—in the Old Testament He used Balaam's donkey to communicate to the prophet. And yet, He *chooses* to use us. God loves us much more than He does donkeys—we have a living, eternal soul. And someday in eternity God would like to say to every single person, "Well done, My faithful servant, well done."

The way we can hear those words when we reach heaven is to live for Jesus today. Many Christians miss out on the blessing of being sold out for the Lord and walking in *His* victory and carrying *His* cross. Instead, they're burdened by the cross of self or the cross of good works. Their attitude is, "Ohhh, the pain of this burden I must bear for the Lord." But Jesus invited us to come unto Him because His yoke is easy and His burden is *light*.

Where we make our mistake is that we think we must be crucified like Jesus was. But He doesn't want us to be crucified—that was His work on the cross. Our part is to enter into what *He* did on the cross and die to ourselves. That's a heavy-duty thing to be sure, but it's certainly not as hard as dying for the sins of the whole world. Because of Jesus, we can pray, "Thank You, Lord, that You've won the battle for me. I know that the things I'm fighting daily are my own flesh and the little darts of the enemy, but Jesus, You had to go full force against all the sin of the world. Thank You."

The cross that we must bear can bring some pain, but it also brings blessings. The blessings are those that accompany any great victory. So when all looks lost and we're seemingly weighed under a burden—whether the burden is sin, self, or circumstances, we must remember that Jesus Christ is Victor.

He won the battle. He won the war.

Give Him praise! Hallelujah!

This day is sacred to our Lord. Do not grieve, for the joy of the Lord is your strength.

—NEHEMIAH 8:10

Do you know how beautiful it is to be happy? Sometimes we get so wrapped up in our own life that we forget how many unhappy people there are out there looking for the joy only Christians have.

Sometimes I run into these people, and they resent our happiness in the Lord. They say, "These Christians are too happy. They get a bill in the mail and they say, 'Praise God!' They stub their toe and they say, 'Glory!' They pay their taxes and say, 'Thank You, Lord!' These Christians are nuts! Why can't they be depressed like everyone else?"

Sure, we Christians have problems, just like everyone else. But the Christian has a secret that keeps him happy no matter what happens. That secret is that the *joy* of the Lord is our strength.

Do you feel weak? Need some strength? Then go to God for the joy He offers. The worst testimony I can think of is for a believer in Christ to live a joyless life in front of unbelievers. What then is the advantage of being a Christian? What do we have to offer a lost, despairing world if not a reason to rejoice?

The second-worst witness to unbelievers is to try and fake the joy of the Lord. They can see right through that plastic religious smile, so don't even bother. The joy of the Lord is *real* and can't be mustered up through our own strength or efforts. His joy is a *gift* and like all of God's gifts is received by faith.

Don't settle for a life without joy. Life's too short.

46   Come Soon, Lord Jesus

Even so, come, Lord Jesus!

—REVELATION 22:20 NKJV

Jesus is coming soon. He's coming with a net to pick up all His chosen ones. And all His chosen ones are waiting expectantly, not worried about the problems of this life, but patiently looking forward to the appearing of their Lord.

Every night my soul prays, "Lord Jesus, come quickly!" My soul is longing to see my Lord. I get so tired of this world's ridicule of my Jesus. People yell His name as a cuss word or they make fun of God's prized possession—His people.

Meanwhile these people of God are living quiet lives in Jesus, going about their business, but glancing up to the sky every so often with the same prayer, "Maranatha, come soon, Lord. Come soon." These are the people who live for the kingdom of God. They give their money to the poor and to the work of God without remorse. They busy themselves with good works in the name of Christ. They openly share the gospel with those whom God sends. They gladly bear the ridicule of Hollywood and the powerful of this world who resent the innocence of the Christian. These quiet believers raise their children for Christ; they serve their brothers and sisters in the local fellowship; they praise their God in all things; they keep themselves unstained from the spirit of the world.

These are the people of God. The chosen ones. Even now the net is being lowered around them to take them to their eternal home, the home that Jesus has promised to all who believe in Him.

47   Entertaining Angels

Be joyful in hope, patient in affliction, faithful in prayer. Share with God's people who are in need. Practice hospitality.

—ROMANS 12:12,13

If you own a home, how open is it? How available is it for God's use? Would you host a Bible study there? If you picked up a hitchhiker and led him to the Lord, would you take him into your home for a few days to disciple him? Would you share the gospel but withhold your couch, your food, and your bathroom?

Already, I can hear you saying, "Brother, that's not my ministry."

Hey, I'm not asking you to start a halfway house and take in 20 or 30 people. There are people who are called to start "house ministries." That's not what I'm talking about. I just want you to think about your stewardship of your home. Many Christians gladly share their money, their time, and even their talents, but their home is off-limits. And yet by opening our homes, we often entertain angels unaware.

My perspective on this came about when Melody and I opened our home to the people God sent. The people God sent usually were a result of a phone call from the leaders in our church, who would ask us to take in another person. We were still getting calls when we had ten people in three bedrooms. Finally, I got a case of what some people might call "righteous indignation." I called our pastor and said, "We've got 700 people in this church, surely someone else can also make their home available. Why don't you preach a sermon on it?" So he did. It was a good sermon. In it he said, "We don't want to have an official 'Christian house' where we send people who need a home. We want to have 100 Christian houses. It's hard for one person to disciple 20 others, but it's better if we have 20 people disciple 20 others one at a time, in their homes." At the end of the sermon he asked people to volunteer to open their homes when the need arose.

A week later the church called me again. Would I take in another person? It seemed that no one had volunteered to open their home to others. No one. So I suggested that the pastor simply go down the list of people in the church and start asking point-blank, "Will you take a person in your home?" So he did and the result was a great blessing. People couldn't say no to the pastor and so the need was met. The tragedy is that it took a personal call to get Christians to exercise the gift of hospitality.

Hospitality in the Bible is a requirement, not a suggestion. If your home hasn't been open, *do it*. Just take in *one* person. Share the gospel. Disciple them.

Everyone should have enough time and room for somebody on their couch to love. The result will be blessing. A closed home means a closing to certain blessings that will only begin when the door is open to the ones God sends you.

If you open your heart, your home must follow.

The LORD's lovingkindnesses indeed never cease, for His compassions never fail. They are new every morning.

—LAMENTATIONS 3:22,23 NASB

My ministry is about the love of Jesus. He doesn't want to torment anybody, and He doesn't want to see anyone tormented. He doesn't stand around with a huge club ready to bash a few skulls. Instead, He's continually inviting sinners to come to Him, to accept His payment for their sins. To all, He says, "Come unto Me. I'm waiting for you. I'm holding the clock back. It's one minute to twelve and every time it wants to tick, I push it back a minute. I'm waiting for one more to come. And one more, and one more, and one more. Why are you waiting? I died for you. I'm dying for you still. I'm sitting before the Father's throne weeping My heart out for you. Come to Me. There's nothing left in this world for you. It's all gonna turn to dust."

We all know instinctively that what Jesus says is true. There's nothing here for us of real value. If we get loaded tonight, tomorrow we'll come down hard. If we make a lot of money today, we'll lose it tomorrow. If we give ourselves to another person tonight, tomorrow they'll disappoint us. If we have a successful business this year, we'll fold up shop next year. The economy will be good for a while, and then it'll go south. Everywhere we look in this world we see things changing. But Jesus is constant. He never changes—He's always *for* us. He always wants the best.

Come unto Him again and again. He never gets tired of being in our presence. Do we get tired of being in His?

49   Maturing in Jesus

Leaving the elementary teaching about the Christ, let us press on to maturity.

—HEBREWS 6:1 NASB

Some Christians never seem to grow past infancy. They go to all the cool praise services and are eager to hear the latest new teaching, but there they are two, three, four, or five years later and still in their cribs clamoring to be fed or have their diapers changed. They've settled into a kind of spiritual Disneyland—maybe even a Fantasyland—and don't want to leave. Meanwhile God's saying, "Listen, man, there's a whole world of starving people out there who need to hear My Word. Who can I send?"

We *expect* to see a helpless baby in the crib, crying for attention, but when the person crying in the crib is a 300-pound adult, it looks pretty sick. God's saying, "Here, have some steak. You need some *meat*." But the baby is responding, "More milk! Gotta have more milk! Love that milk!" After all, milk is easy to digest. Meat takes some energy to turn into muscle and bone.

God keeps calling the babies to get up and walk, to get out of their cribs and start to meet other people's needs instead of waiting to have their own infantile needs met. God's calling us to *go*. Some who are still on a milk diet should already be out on the field in ministry.

Paul faced the same problem in Corinth. He told them that they were still drinking milk when they should be eating meat.

Folks, there was a lot of work that needed doing in Corinth. Sexual immorality plagued the church. There were divisions among the brethren. Just when Paul needed to see some maturity, he found infancy. The same is happening today. The needs are great but the workers are few. This doesn't mean that we should run off half-cocked and do something just for the sake of getting busy—but even *that's* better than doing nothing.

A happy life is really easy to have. First, we have to grow up in the Lord. Second, find out what work God has set aside for us to do. Third, *do it*.

*Do nothing out of selfish ambition or vain conceit, but
in humility consider others better than yourselves.*

—PHILIPPIANS 2:3

The test of a Christian is whether or not we love one another.
In our flesh we can *like* one another. We can lend a friend some
money, take him to the movie, give him a ride to work, buy him
a birthday present—all that we can do in our natural strength—
but that's not the love that proves our Christianity. No, the love
God is looking for is the love that lays down its life for the other
person. The love that's willing to *die* so that another may live.

That kind of love is impossible in the natural and only possible
in the supernatural. It's only available through the Holy Spirit
living in us. We all know this is true. Selfishness isn't taught; it's
inbred. *Un*-selfishness has to be taught. We're born selfish creatures. We want our bottle of milk *now*. We want our rattle *now*.
We don't care if Mommy is tired and taking a nap; we want her to
wait on us *now*.

Put two two-year-olds and a Hershey bar in a room and see
what happens. Or remember when your mom took the chocolate
chip cookies out of the oven and gave you two of them with the
instructions to give one to your brother? One of these cookies is
bigger than the other and has twice as many chocolate chips. So
on the way to your brother, you look at those cookies and your
mouth is watering. You *love* chocolate chip cookies. Of course
you're a Christian, you go to Sunday school every week. And
God's saying to you, "Give your brother the larger cookie." And
you answer, "But God, these are *chocolate chip* cookies—my
favorite."

Today, we're grown up and still we struggle with our selfishness—if we're honest enough to admit it. We want what we want and we want it as soon as possible. Sometimes we might even find a way to put a religious spin on our selfish desires. "Uh, God, I feel really led to go out with this non-Christian. Maybe if we date, I can share the gospel or let them see how neat it is to be a Christian."

There are lots of ways we try to rationalize what we really want to do by putting a Christian label on it. But God isn't fooled. He knew the motives of Peter's heart *before* he selfishly denied the Lord three times. And He knows all our attempts to cover our sin or whitewash it with religiosity. He knows that we all have a master's degree in selfishness. Still, He's patient with us, showing us our fleshly attitudes and at the same time offering us the power of His Holy Spirit to love as we should. He knows there's no other way to live for others than by the Holy Spirit.

He knows and He continually wants us to know too.

51   Be Filled with the Holy Spirit

*After they prayed, the place where they were meeting
was shaken. And they were all filled with the Holy
Spirit and spoke the word of God boldly.*

—ACTS 4:31

Remember when Peter was in the boat and Jesus was out trucking across the water? Peter called out, "Lord, is that You? If it's really You, tell me to come out and walk on the water too."

Jesus replied, "Yes, Peter, it's Me. Come on out on the water."

So Peter steps out of the boat and all the disciples think, *Boy, I wish I'd have done that.* So he starts to walk across the water and then as he takes his eyes off Jesus and looks at the water...glub, glub, glub. All the disciples are thinking, *Boy, I'm glad I didn't do that.*

Good old Peter. Later he told Jesus he'd die for Him. He even cut off the ear of the high priest's slave when they come to arrest Jesus. Peter was hot stuff for the Lord...until Jesus was taken away. Then Peter's true character was revealed—he was a sniveling coward. He not only denied the Lord, but cursed Him. "No, I never knew that so-and-so." Only he didn't use the words "so-and-so."

Then he looked over and saw Jesus coming with the guards. The cock crowed three times. It was then that Peter saw who he was without Jesus. He saw that he didn't have the power to be the man he was supposed to be. He was just like any other guy—looking out for number one.

The Gospels single out Peter for his betrayal, but we don't exactly see any of the other disciples rushing in to stand up for Jesus. Where were they? Why didn't they speak up? Because they too were cowards when Jesus was taken from them. And then they all watched in horror, no doubt, as Jesus was mocked, stood trial, and was given a criminal's death. These guys must have been devastated. What had these past three years been about anyway?

But wait. That's not the end of the story. Jesus triumphed over death and "appeared to the disciples." They may have given up on Him, but Jesus still loved them in spite of their cowardice. He then "breathed on them" and said, "Receive ye the Holy Ghost." He then told them to wait in Jerusalem until they were clothed with power from on high. Then He ascended into heaven.

So all the disciples and a bunch of other followers of Jesus were in the upper room, with the door locked, shivering and fearful, complaining, "We're in big trouble. They're gonna cut us up into little pieces." Then it says that all of a sudden the room was filled with a mighty rushing wind and "they were all filled with the Holy Spirit."

And what happened? These same sniveling cowards went out of the upper room, down into the streets, and preached the gospel like bold lions. That very day 3,000 souls were saved! The day started off with 500 believers and ended with 3,500!

Do you see what happens when the Holy Spirit comes? Christians get changed and non-Christians get saved. It's been 2,000 years since the day of Pentecost, but the Holy Spirit is still here, still turning cowards into raging lions for the gospel.

It's great to be a follower of Jesus. But if we really want to be His disciple, let's get filled and stay filled with the Holy Spirit. Let's believe God that He can work with the likes of us—poor useless flunkies, sinking deeper into the water, hopeless apart from Jesus.

We are citizens of heaven, where the Lord Jesus Christ lives.

—PHILIPPIANS 3:20 NLT

Have you ever thought of how much Jesus gave up for us? He not only gave up His life, but in order to come to earth and save us, He gave up living in heaven for 33 years. That may not make much of an impression on us now because we don't know what heaven's like, but someday we'll see. Someday we'll go, "Wow, Jesus, You gave up all *this* to come to *earth* for *me?*"

And then we'll realize that this wonderful place—heaven— this home with God—is ours *forever*. We never have to leave heaven once we're there. And because Jesus died once for sins for all time—He will be with us forever.

Although we see heaven through a glass darkly because we're still housed in this fleshly body, Paul tells us that we're already citizens of heaven. We're already *there* by virtue of Jesus' promise. We need to look past our flesh that so easily disappoints us and see our home in heaven. We need to see that Book of Life where our name is *already written*. Just a glimpse of what we have waiting for us will get us through any kind of junk Satan can throw at us.

Praise God, heaven is my home!

53 We All Have Problems

He who conceals his transgressions will not prosper, but he who confesses and forsakes them will find compassion.

—PROVERBS 28:13 NASB

God wants us to be real. There's no room for phoniness in the Christian life. No pasted-on smiles, please. No living in denial if you've got a serious problem. Too many of us keep secrets—even from the Lord, if that were possible. We don't want to face the fact that we aren't the perfect Christian witness or that we're going through a trial that might embarrass us if anyone knew about it. So we learn to put up the facade of faith. All the while our hearts are aching from the secrets we're keeping. These secrets fester in our hearts and will ultimately wreck our faith, if not our health.

Hiding our problems is like trying to smuggle a small dog on an airplane by stuffing it under your coat. You're afraid the little guy's gonna start barking any minute and give away the secret, or that by holding him so tightly you'll smother him. Or imagine walking into a dark room and pretending that it's full of light. You can pretend all you want, but eventually you'll bump into something and knock it over. The secret will come out.

The way to deal with our problems—and we all have them, so stop pretending you don't—is to first get real with God about the problem. Admit to God that you are powerless and have no answer to this trial. Then seek the help of someone who's in a position to help you. It may or may not be a pastor. It might be a ministry raised up by God for your very problem. In these last days God has graciously raised up many people and ministries to address any secret sin or problem imaginable. You *can* find release and healing.

No matter what your problem is, *keep seeking help until you get it!* And after you've come out the other side—restored, healthy, and strong—don't be surprised if God uses you to comfort others in the same affliction.

54   Jesus Alone Is Worthy

You were bought at a price; do not become slaves of men.

—1 CORINTHIANS 7:23

Andraé Crouch told me once that he couldn't go to church much anymore. When I asked him why not, he told me that at church he just wants to be fed and to worship the Lord. Instead, he has to deal with people who want his autograph or to tell him about a song they wrote or to just be in his presence. When he did go to church, he had to sit in the back and sneak out as soon as the service was over. He just couldn't take it anymore, so he had to start having church at home by inviting a few friends who really loved the Lord and would just come and worship God with him.

I was reminded of this when I got a letter from a guy who attended the Christian rock festival I played at in Pennsylvania. There were about 40,000 people there and several performers. This letter I got just broke my heart. The guy said, "Keith, before I came to the Lord, I had idols. I idolized KISS, Olivia Newton-John, John Denver…stars like that. I covered my walls with their posters, bought all their records, and looked up to them as heroes…superstars. Then when I became a Christian, I just switched idols. There were still posters on my wall, but now they were posters of B. J. Thomas, Chuck Girard, Barry McGuire, and The 2nd Chapter of Acts. There was really no difference in my idolatry. Nobody told me it should be any different."

The reason the guy was writing was because of what happened at that concert in Pennsylvania. I got up on the stage to do my music and saw that there were people out there rollin' in the aisle, screaming…not for Jesus…but for the performers. They were like groupies. So I started playing my music, and I felt God say, "Look, man, I've heard all your tunes. Why don't you worship Me? These people need to know how to worship Me." So I spent the next whole hour leading worship. It was great: 35,000 pairs of hands in the air—70,000 hands altogether—raised in worship to the Lord. The Spirit of God started to move as we praised Him. I'll never forget that concert.

The guy's letter continued, "You talked about Jesus being the only star that night, so when I came home I tore down all the posters from my walls. I decided to give God the glory. But Keith, if you hadn't said that, I probably would have put your poster up on the wall too."

We need to get it straight: God is no respecter of persons. He loves the drunk in the gutter as much as He loves Billy Graham or Barry McGuire or Andraé Crouch—or anybody. We're all His favorite sons and daughters, and He saves us all. It's not His will that any should perish.

We should never exalt *people*. For one thing, they may let us down someday. For another, we always get it wrong. We foolishly exalt some loser like Keith Green and ignore the little old lady working in the soup kitchen in Indiana who's been feeding the poor for years.

Let God lift up whom He wants to. Because when God lifts up a person, Jesus Christ is exalted. He alone is worthy.

*Do not fear, for I am with you; do not be dismayed,
for I am your God. I will strengthen and help you. I
will uphold you with my righteous right hand.*

—ISAIAH 41:10

Being on the road for weeks at a time is sometimes kind of weird. It's a lot of work, and you never know what the results will be. I just got back from a nine-week concert tour around the country and I'm pretty tired. But what was interesting on this trip was that I went to some places where they'd never heard of me and the audience was small—maybe only 20 people, and then I'd go to places where there were lots of people who were really enthusiastic about me being there. At the end of the concert, when I gave an altar call, sometimes only one person would come forward. At other times, quite a few responded. But numbers don't really matter.

I remember at one of the smaller concerts, only one girl came forward, and as I sat at the end of the stage talking to her, I told her, "You're the whole reason why I came to this town." And that's true. God wanted her *saved*. And I was blessed to be able to deliver the message and pray with her. Ministering to only *one* person is worth the whole concert tour because Jesus would have suffered the agony of the cross for only one person.

Later in the tour I played at Fort Leonard Wood army base in Missouri. There were about 500 young raw recruits there, all about 18 years old. Their hair was cut really short, and they were still pretty nervous about being in the army. Under their breath, they were all saying, "I want my mommy."

After the concert I gave an invitation and about 350 of them came forward to accept Christ. They told me, "Man, I really need *something* to get me through this." Yeah, I know what they mean. They were going through boot camp and it was kind of rough on them. But boot camp in the army is really a lot like life. We're all soldiers going through boot camp and sometimes we go through experiences that make us cry, "I want my mommy." Almost every day we have to walk the obstacle course set before us. We have to dodge the bullets of the enemy and we have to guard our victory with diligence.

But rest easy. Daddy's here. Our Father knows all about the boot camp we're in. He's the Commander-in-Chief, and nothing's going to happen to us that He hasn't got a handle on. Even today there may be some heavy fire in your direction, but it's okay; we're soldiers on the *winning* side.

God is light; in him there is no darkness at all. If we claim to have fellowship with him yet walk in the darkness, we lie and do not live by the truth.

—1 JOHN 1:5,6

If you've ever been inside an old Gothic church, you can't help but notice the beauty of the stained glass windows. They're at their best, though, when the light outside is bright and can pour through the windows into the sanctuary. That's when the colors are their truest and the message of the window is most impressive.

But later in the day, when the sun sets and the darkness descends, the beautiful deep greens and blues start turning reddish green and reddish blue. As darkness deepens, the stained glass, so beautiful only hours before, turns black.

That's like us. We're like God's stained glass windows—fantastic to behold when His light is shining through us—a true work of the Creator's art. But when we allow darkness to pour through us, His light leaves, and we become drab and dark. The beauty that's in us is still there, but no one can see it.

There's darkness around us all the time, but we don't have to let it affect us. God's light is also around us all the time and we can choose to let His light showcase His creation. The sun never has to set in the life of a Christian.

Stained Glass

We are like windows,
Stained with colors of the rainbow,
Set in a darkened room,
Till the Bridegroom comes to shine through,
Then the colors fall around our feet,

Over those we meet,
Covering all the gray that we see,
Rainbow colors of assorted hues,
Come exchange your blues,
For His love that you see shining through me.

We are His daughters and sons,
We are the colorful ones,
We are the kids of the King,
Rejoice in everything.

My colors grow so dim,
When I start to fall away from Him,
But up comes the strongest wind
That He sends to blow me back
Into His arms again.

And the colors fall around my feet,
Over those I meet,
Changing all the gray that I see,
Rainbow colors of the risen Son,
Reflect the One,
The One who came to set us all free.

We are His daughters and sons,
We are the colorful ones,
We are the kids of the King,
Rejoice in everything.

We are like windows,
Stained with colors of the rainbow,
No longer set in a darkened room,
'Cause the Bridegroom wants to shine through you,
No longer set in a darkened room,
'Cause the Bridegroom wants to shine through you.

But a Samaritan, as he traveled, came where the man
was; and when he saw him, he took pity on him. He
went to him and bandaged his wounds, pouring on oil
and wine. Then he put the man on his own donkey,
took him to an inn and took care of him.

—LUKE 10:33,34

Lately I've been studying *agape* love—you know, the kind of love that comes from God. And while I've been studying it, I've also been giving concerts around the country in lots of different churches. And one thing I've noticed is that this supernatural kind of *agape* love is missing from most churches—including the one I go to. Oh, there's always a few people who walk in this kind of love, but not enough to make the kind of difference the church should be making.

Our love is too shallow. We pat each other on the back, maybe even give someone a hug and say, "Praise God, brother!" but we don't seem to move beyond that. And if we walk into church and we see someone sitting there looking kind of depressed, we move on, thinking, *I don't want to sit next to him.* So we try to find the one that everyone loves to sit next to because they're happy and maybe even good-looking. Meanwhile, the unlovely members of the body—the unattractive ones, the overweight ones, the miserable ones, the lonely ones—are left behind. And their loneliness breeds more loneliness. Depression breeds more depression.

Agape love seeks out the hurting. It sought us out when we cried to God for help. And when God saved us, He planted His love in our hearts like a seed. But we don't let it grow. We're too occupied with the shallow love that's friendly with others, but which has narrow boundaries—comfortable boundaries. Meanwhile that seed of *agape* love is trying to push up through the concrete in our heart. It aches to be so much a part of our life that we seek out the hurting and pour God's love on the wounded like Mary Magdalene poured the expensive perfume over Jesus.

Let's let the *agape* love of God consume us. Let's set aside the shallow religious love that only wants to be around the attractive, the happy, the unneedy.

58   It's Fruit Inspection Time

A good tree cannot bear bad fruit, and a bad tree
cannot bear good fruit. Every tree that does not bear
good fruit is cut down and thrown into the fire. Thus,
by their fruit you will recognize them.

—MATTHEW 7:18-20

All the good deeds you can do between now and Doomsday won't count for a thing unless they're done in Jesus. You can open up halfway houses and soup kitchens and prison ministries and homes for unwed mothers and all kinds of things, but unless Jesus is doing it through you, they count for nothing in the eyes of God.

You can't get to heaven by working and doing good deeds, but once you meet Jesus, you can't be a growing Christian without serving others. You don't plant a peach tree and expect to see peaches the next day. You plant the tree when it's just a little stick with a burlap ball of roots at the bottom. You plant it, you pat down the soil around it, you water it, you weed it, you prune it, you watch it grow, and in about three years or so you expect to see some peaches on it.

Maybe one spring you come out and see buds forming on the tree and you think, *Oh boy, now I'm gonna see some peaches.* But then the buds fall off. So you wait till next year and the same thing happens. You're starting to get a little mad. You take out that little cardboard thing from the drawer that hung on the stick when you planted it, to see if you've done anything wrong. But no, you did everything right. There must be something wrong with the tree.

That's the way Jesus looks at us. He's patient with us but after a while He comes looking for peaches—for fruit.

Think about it in your own life. How fruitful are you? Are there peaches on the tree yet? Are you leading others to the Lord? Serving others in some capacity?

Some Christians mistakenly think that it's the pastor's job to lead others to the Lord, but a pastor is like a shepherd, and it's the sheep who bear other sheep, not the shepherd. If you bought a herd of sheep and three years later their numbers hadn't increased, you'd want to sell them or turn them into lamb chops, because they're no good at being reproductive sheep, expanding the herd.

How did you come to the Lord? Did someone love you enough to witness to you or to invite you to their fellowship? Did someone encourage you, show you how to be a Christian?

Today take some time to have a fruit inspection of your own life. If there are no peaches, then figure out why not and commit yourself to being useful to God.

59   The Road Is Often Bumpy

*I am the least of the apostles and do not even deserve
to be called an apostle, because I persecuted the church
of God. But by the grace of God I am what I am, and
his grace to me was not without effect.*

—1 CORINTHIANS 15:9,10

Don't ever let anyone tell you that by becoming a Christian all your troubles will disappear. Some troubles will be gone, that's for sure. Troubles like guilt and lack of peace—those should be gone from the life of the Christian. But other problems will arrive to take their place, the most common of which is probably persecution from your family and friends.

Some problems you had before you were a Christian might stay with you a while—or even forever. If your parents or family were messed up, they're not going to change just because you became a Christian. In fact, your family's problems may get worse unless they come to the Lord too.

When Jesus comes into your heart, the road begins. It's a great road with a fantastic destination, but it has some bumps along the way and a few uphill twists and turns. The road isn't always smooth. Don't expect it to be. But all through the ride, you get some great compensation for your trouble. You have the Lord Jesus inside you, and you have lots of brothers and sisters to encourage you. Some of them have gone around that same hairpin curve in the road you're facing and they will help you.

Too many young believers fall away when trouble comes because they were told that being a Christian would be a piece of cake and that their problems would disappear. But what they should have been told is that being a Christian will bring victory as they go *through* their problems. They should be told that maturity as a Christian is a process that takes some time. *There is no such thing as instant Christian maturity.*

The reason to become a Christian isn't to solve your problems. It's because you see that *you* are your biggest problem. You've failed at being who you know God created you to be. You hunger for a relationship with God that will allow you to become like Him. To be honest, I became a Christian because I couldn't stand Keith Green without Him.

When you come to God that way, it doesn't really matter about your circumstantial problems. Your biggest problem is solved—that of *yourself.*

*This day I call heaven and earth as witnesses against
you that I have set before you life and death, blessings
and curses. Now choose life, so that you and your
children may live.*

—DEUTERONOMY 30:19

Christianity isn't a bunch of "don'ts." Believing in Jesus isn't a
list of things you have to give up. No doubt if you have a real
born-again experience with God, there are certain things you *will*
give up, but the giving up of them is a fruit of salvation, not a
means to being saved.

One thing you'll give up is hell. Once you're saved, hell no
longer has any claim on you. It no longer is your eternal destination, and the devil, who had been your father before you were
saved is no longer a relative. God is now your Father and heaven
is your home.

When you give up hell's claim on your life, you'll also give up
depression, despair, loneliness, bitterness—all that junk that the
devil has been laying on you during your unsaved years. As these
things fall away, you'll pick up the habits of heaven—there will
be joy, peace, purpose, and power to live right.

See how hard it is to be a Christian? You trade all the stuff that
destroys you for all the good stuff that blesses you. That's really
hard, isn't it?

For some people, it must be. They don't want to accept Christ
and His peace. They'd honestly rather be miserable. It's like an
addiction. Their anger, depression, and bitterness have been
with them so long, they really don't want to give them up. When
a person reaches that state, it's really a tragedy. What hope is
there for a person who treasures his or her misery?

Sadly, some Christians are the same way. They bring their fleshly misery from their old life into their new life. Sometimes it's because they got a lot of attention by being miserable. They could get sympathy from friends, a shoulder to cry on, and they don't want to ruin a good thing.

The thing is, when a person chooses to live in hell, God gives them their choice. God doesn't drag anybody into heaven, like "C'mon, you're gonna be saved whether you like it or not. Now get in here and grab a harp!" Neither does God throw anyone into hell. Everyone in hell has chosen their destination.

We've chosen heaven, so let's let heaven rule our lives while we're here on earth. Lay down your depression and pick up the garment of praise. Set aside all bitterness and take up joy. Trade your anger for blessing. Live by heaven.

*Judge nothing before the appointed time; wait till the
Lord comes. He will bring to light what is hidden in
darkness and will expose the motives of men's hearts.
At that time each will receive his praise from God.*
—1 CORINTHIANS 4:5

A day is coming when we can no longer choose our destiny, a
day when all the choices are locked in for eternity. Each tick of
the clock brings that day one second closer. Every day that
passes, every hour that goes by, God watches the events on earth.
And one day enough will be enough. The stench of our pornography and violence and all the abominable actions that repulse
God will reach their fill.

God's eyes are in all places at all times. Nothing is hidden
from Him. His eyes see every single pornographic magazine that's
published. God is seeing every pornographic film being shown
right now. He's watching every girl who is being raped right now,
every young boy being molested. He sees every murder being
committed.

Does this sound gross to you? Turn your stomach? How then
do you think God feels? Don't you think He has emotions? If
God beholds the falling of a sparrow, do you think He has no
opinion when a child is violated? Our God is not the metaphysical god of the cults who watches passively without emotion
when tragedy occurs. Our God is not the god of the heathen,
fashioned out of rock or stone.

As God is moved by sin, we should be too. The gospel we've
believed *must* send us into this world of increasing sin and
lawlessness. The molested boy, the raped girl, the pornography
addict are all held captive by an enemy. Both they *and their*

perpetrators still have a short time before the door is closed for all time. We have the message of life, of restoration, of healing. But brothers—sisters—let's *redeem the time, for the days are evil and time is short!*

I have this against you, that you have left your first love.

—REVELATION 2:4 NASB

One day God allowed me to see what my rank heart was really like. I was disgusted with what I saw. I had been a Christian for a year or two, I had sung all the praise songs, knew the official Christianese words, knew the right people—I even had a hit record album. But in spite of my knowledge, my friends, and my success, my heart told me I was a Pharisee.

I had an outer shell that projected my religiosity, but inside I was a scared little boy. God knew it, and now I knew it too. It doesn't take long for a new Christian to get sidetracked into religious performance. What had begun as a joyful conversion was morphing into yet another fruitless Christian. I was dealing with some of the same problems that I'd had for years. Eyes that had wept for the lost were now dry. What happened? Why did it happen?

It's the same thing that happens to a lot of Christians—we move away from our first love. The things we do out of joy when we were first Christians become habit. Our prayers, once uttered out of a full heart of faith, become lifeless exercises in doubt.

In God's mercy, He lets us see how we've strayed. He constantly woos us back to that "first love" experience. When we see the dryness of our eyes issuing from our even drier hearts, we can rejoice that God is calling us back to Him.

He won't let us be satisfied with dead religion.

My Eyes Are Dry

My eyes are dry,
My faith is old,
My heart is hard,
My prayers are cold,
And I know how
I ought to be,
Alive to You,
And dead to me.

Oh, what can be done,
For an old heart like mine,
Soften it up,
With oil and wine.
The oil is You,
Your Spirit of love,
Please wash me anew,
In the wine of Your blood.

My eyes are dry,
My faith is old,
My heart is hard,
My prayers are cold,
And I know how
I ought to be,
Alive to You,
And dead to me.

63   Let's Not Turn Our Heads

A poor widow came and put in two very small copper coins, worth only a fraction of a penny. Calling his disciples to him, Jesus said, "I tell you the truth, this poor widow has put more into the treasury than all the others."

—MARK 12:42,43

Today there are starving people in America. Some are starving for new spiritual life in Jesus and others are literally starving for food. There are kids in our ghettos going to bed hungry. There are babies with alcoholic dads who spend the little money they get on liquor. There are moms who would give anything for some Hamburger Helper.

We see ads on TV for organizations that feed the hungry. They show us cute little kids with bloated bellies and we shake our heads and say, "Awww, isn't that terrible. Please pass the popcorn."

Then the ad asks us to send them some money to help feed these kids, and maybe we'll mentally figure out if we can afford it from our surplus. But God gives our surplus to be returned to Him, so when we give out of our surplus we're only giving what belongs to God anyway. If you *really* want to be a giver, try giving out of your sustenance, after your surplus has already been returned to God.

Think about how much money you spent on concerts, music, and entertainment last year and compare it with how much you gave to the poor. Right away, you go into defense mode—"Gotta find an excuse, gotta find a way to rationalize it." So you turn to the Scripture and find the verse that says, "the poor you'll always have with you." And you think, *There, that's it. The poor will always be with us. I can't change that.*

Meanwhile God looks at American Christians, with all their wealth and their constant talk about money and the stock market and the economy, and He thinks, *You, of all the Christians down through history, have the power to save a few of My children from starving, and instead you're out looking at bigger television sets.*

The test of a Christian is if we obey God. We can repeat the sinner's prayer a thousand times, but if our hearts don't get broken by the things that break God's heart, how can we then be saved? Sometimes I walk into a Christian bookstore and expect to see the number one best-seller be a book called *How to Do Your Own Thing in the Center of God's Will* by Luke W. Warm. If there were such a book, it would be fiction. There's no way to do your own thing and do God's thing at the same time.

Becoming a Christian means giving up your desires for His. It means seeing the poor, hungry, and hurting through His eyes. It means committing your material assets to Him in any way that seems right to Him. Our attitude shouldn't be, "How much do I have to give to God this week?" It should be, "How much should I keep for my needs this week?"

If God doesn't have our wallets, He doesn't have our hearts.

A Billion Starving People

I find it hard to turn away
A billion starving people
But what can one do
I've heard you say
You can save someone's life

I wanna save a life today
I wanna get someone close with my Father
Feed them the Bread of Life today
I wanna help them to get stronger
And help them last longer
And give them a chance to see Jesus

I find it hard to just ignore
The murdered unborn children
Yes times have changed but still God warns
You shall not take a life

I wanna save a life today
I wanna keep one alive for my Father
Who will avenge the blood
Of weak and helpless ones someday
Whose lives are spilled out like water
Lambs in the slaughter
And each one is handmade by Jesus

I find it hard to turn away
A billion starving people
A billion starving people

64   The Right Kind of Treasure

*As He was setting out on a journey, a man ran up to
Him and knelt before Him, and asked Him, "Good
Teacher, what shall I do to inherit eternal life?"*

—MARK 10:17 NASB

The rich young ruler had a lot going for him. He came to Jesus interested in gaining eternal life. He came in broad daylight, unlike Nicodemus, who slyly came at night so he wouldn't be seen. The rich guy kneels at Jesus' feet and asks for eternal life.

Wow. That's pretty neat. Rich, young, probably good-looking, and quite a moral young man—he's kept the commandments from his youth. Hey, this guy is a perfect candidate for almost any church in America. He'd be a real trophy for Christ, wouldn't he?

Almost any evangelist today would whip out a tract and start to lead the guy in the sinner's prayer. And the rich young ruler would probably pray it. Five minutes later he'd get the glad hand of fellowship and presto, the guy is saved. Give him a tithing envelope and start making plans for the new building.

But Jesus didn't quite know how to witness to the guy correctly. He asked the guy about keeping the law, of all things. And when the young man replied that he had kept the law, Jesus told him there was just one more thing he had to do to receive eternal life: "Go and sell everything you own, give it to the poor, then come and follow Me, then you shall have treasures in heaven."

Ouch.

At these words the rich young ruler went away *sad* for he had many possessions. I think the rich young ruler understood fully what Jesus was asking. He *believed* Jesus. After all, why else would he go away "sad"? If he didn't believe Jesus was telling the truth, then what's the big deal? He could go away thinking this Jesus guy was full of beans. No, this guy was *convicted*.

Jesus didn't chase after him though. He let "the big one" get away. He wasn't going to make deals with anyone. It was all or nothing for the rich young ruler. Jesus wanted the young man in his entirety. It wasn't that Jesus rejected the guy. He invited him to join Him. It just turned out that Jesus was asking too much—everything. That's what He wants of us too. *Everything*.

Jesus says to each person, "Give Me all or nothing. I want your whole life or forget it." But when we make that decision to follow Him with our whole hearts, we receive a compensation that surpasses the anything we gave up.

Too bad the rich young ruler didn't realize that.

*The King will reply, "I tell you the truth, whatever you
did for one of the least of these brothers of mine, you
did for me."*

—MATTHEW 25:40

I heard an interview on the radio the other day with this new
singer named Amy Grant. During the interview, she humbly told
about a dream she'd had recently. Amy said she was in heaven,
standing before Jesus, and He asked her, "Amy, My daughter,
what are you doing on earth for Me?" Amy said she pulled out
her new record album, this flat circular piece of black plastic, and
said, "Look, Jesus." And right then she noticed that the record
was melting all over her hand and running down her arm. Every
Christian musician certainly understands her dream and fears
the same thing.

I sure understand it. All my music is only a tool. In itself it
has no eternal value and will one day be ashes. Our bodies are
tools too, given to us to be used in the service of God. But too
often we wear out our body by letting it run down stretched out
in front of a TV set, instead of actively serving on the mission
field or in the soup kitchen or on the hard streets of our decay-
ing cities. We feed our bodies more than we burn off in work
and so we get fat. We're literally weighed down by the gravity
of our fleshly appetites. Meanwhile we're doing nothing for the
Lord.

The word "do" is so important. Think about what the Bible
would be like without the word "do." Jesus thought "do" was a
pretty important word. He asks us, "Why *do* you call Me Lord,
Lord, and not *do* what I say?"

The greatest portion of Scripture on the word "do" is Matthew 25:31-46. You've all read it before. Read it again today. Think about what in your life is like the black plastic record that you would offer to Jesus—and see it melt into nothing.

Work for the things that are eternal, not temporal.

If I speak in the tongues of men and of angels, but have not love, I am only a resounding gong or a clanging cymbal.

—1 CORINTHIANS 13:1

There are four things you've got to do if you want to follow Jesus. First, you must have fellowship. And I don't mean just going to church. It must be more than that. In the army, when you go into basic training, they put you in with other army members. And when they station you, they station you with other army members. Can you imagine how inefficient the army would be if every soldier was stationed with a civilian? You'd soon lose the cohesiveness with your army brothers and sisters that's so important to the success of the military. So too Christians have a cohesiveness that must be maintained for spiritual health. My advice is to live with other Christians, play with other Christians, and work with other Christians—even if it means less pay than a job with all non-Christians.

Second, read the Word. The Bible is your *food*. It's not a duty; it's nourishment. Can you imagine if you ate your meals as a duty—"Well, I guess I better force myself to sit down and eat this steak and these mashed potatoes and the hot fudge sundae for dessert."

Why then do we say to ourselves, "Well, I guess I better force myself to read five chapters from Proverbs today"? If you're not used to reading the Bible daily, start in the New Testament with the book of John. Choose a translation that doesn't have a lot of "thees" and "thous" in it—unless you're used to speaking Elizabethan English.

Third is prayer. God doesn't want you to *say* your prayers. He wants to see you *live by prayer.* Twice in the New Testament we're reminded of this. Paul says we're to "pray without ceasing" and to "pray at all times in the Spirit." That means not just in the morning, or just at your bedside, or before meals, but anywhere, anytime. On the job, driving your car (just don't close your eyes!), anywhere and everywhere. Remember too that prayer isn't a shopping list for heaven's store—"Lord, I want a new bike; Lord, I need a new girlfriend; Lord, I want a ministry..." Try that on Santa Claus, not God. At least half of prayer is listening, not speaking.

The fourth thing is to become a big mouth for Jesus. We have Youth for Christ, Youth With A Mission, Campus Crusade for Christ—how about Big Mouths for Jesus?

So many Christians only want to witness when they feel "led" or "called" to share with a person. But Jesus said, "Go into all nations, preach the gospel to every creature." That means we need to witness with our mouths *and our lives.* If you have a bumper sticker on your car, that's fine. Just make sure your life (and your driving) back up your bumper's message.

God looks for us to preach the gospel and live the gospel unashamedly. Open your mouth for Jesus. Let your life back up the words your mouth speaks by the way you love. Otherwise you're a clanging cymbal.

Because you are lukewarm, and neither cold nor hot,
I will vomit you out of My mouth.

—Revelation 3:16 NKJV

For a long time I didn't understand why Jesus said He'd rather us be freezing cold than lukewarm. He says, "I wish you were hot or cold, but since you're lukewarm I'm going to spit you out of My mouth." Whoa, Jesus, why would You want me cold rather than lukewarm? After all, warm is closer to hot than cold.

But then I finally got it. It was like Jesus said, "When you're lukewarm, that means you say you're a Christian, but you don't act like one. That means the world looks at you and says, 'You represent Jesus. What a farce Jesus must be.' "

That's why He'd rather us be cold. When we're cold, we don't go around saying, "I represent Jesus"; we go around asking, "Where's the party?"

Not only does the lukewarm Christian get spit out of the mouth of Jesus, but there's nobody on this planet more miserable than the tepid Christian. He's too much of a Christian to enjoy his sin and too worldly to enjoy Jesus. So he sits on the fence thinking, *What a boring life. I'm either going to a party or to church and enjoying neither one.*

Jesus created us in such a way that our enjoyment comes from full surrender to Him. To the extent that we're still satisfied by the world, we're dissatisfied with Jesus. We're like a bride in her bridal chamber preparing for the wedding, but thinking, *I don't know if I really want to marry this guy.*

Get it settled. Are you hot or cold? Choose one or the other, but don't be lukewarm.

*Beckon yourselves to be dead indeed to sin, but alive
to God in Christ Jesus our Lord.*

—ROMANS 6:11 NKJV

Do you know what "holy" means? It means completely, utterly,
spotlessly *white*. Pure. Not a speck of dirt. Untouched. Un-
perverted. Unwrinkled. *Perfect*. And we say—quite truthfully—
"That's not me. I can't be that way."

Neither can I. Not in a billion years. But Jesus can be that way.
He *is* that way. And if He lives in me, I can walk in His holiness,
not my own. We still sin, but it's not a conscious choosing of sin.
The difference can be explained like this: It's the difference
between a guy breaking into your house and stealing your TV set
versus him knocking on your door saying, "Hello, I'm your
burglar. I'm here for the TV and anything else of value." If you
respond, "Oh hi, come on in. The TV is over there in the corner,
and I'll go get my diamond cuff links for you. Can I help you carry
the TV out?" that's like consciously sinning. Allowing yourself to
get ripped off by the enemy is to choose sin. But the sins we
unconsciously commit are done without our open consent.

The blood of Jesus covers both, but if we want holiness, the
choosing of sin must cease as we reckon ourselves dead to sin.
Not only do we have the holiness of Jesus in us, but we also were
crucified with Him on the cross, and that part of us that helps
the burglar carry out the TV, the part of us that chooses sin, is
now dead. In Romans 6 Paul tells us the way to victory: *Reckon
yourselves dead to sin and alive to Christ Jesus*.

Don't try to put yourself to death; it can't be done. Rather
reckon His death as your death and His resurrection as your resurrection. That's the only way to ensure victory.

69   Kiss the Devil Goodbye

*Submit yourselves, then, to God. Resist the devil, and
he will flee from you.*

—JAMES 4:7

Do you know what a "Dear John" letter is? It's the nickname for
the kind of letter a lot of soldiers got during World War II. Their
girlfriends back home found a new guy while they were away and
so they wrote their guys basically saying, "It's over. I found someone new. Sorry." It broke a lot of GI hearts to receive a letter like
that.

Shortly after I became a Christian, God showed me that I
needed to write a "Dear John" letter. My letter though was
directed to the devil, and it informed him that our relationship
was over because I found someone new. Someone better. I told
him, "Listen man, you and I were once big buddies, you know,
but it's all over now, Big D."

Maybe you need to write a letter like that to the devil. Does
he know that it's over between the two of you? I wrote a song
that might help you compose your own letter.

Dear John Letter (To the Devil)

Oh, I used to love you, but now that's hard to do
'Cause I got some information
'Bout them evil things at night that you do.
Now the whole thing is through. We're through!
Oh, you're such a devil
How'd you get me to believe you were true?

Oh my momma warned me, and how my daddy cried
The day I left my home

You said you'd always keep me satisfied
But oh, how you lied. You lied!
Well, I should have heard my momma's words
But then I guess I had too much pride. Original sin!

I used to lie awake at night
And see your face on the ceiling,
Oh, what a bad feeling I have
When I think of how you almost got me
In the ways of the world. In the ways of the world.

My so-called friends say I've misjudged you
My anger's all in vain
But I'm afraid you got to them
Before I had a chance to explain
And it caused me such pain. Ouch!
'Cause they were such good friends of mine
But now you've got them
Playing your game. You creep!

Oh I used to lie awake at night
And see your face on the ceiling,
What a bad feeling I have
When I think of how you almost got me
In the ways of the world. In the ways of the world.

Well, I believe in Jesus
And what He said He's gonna do.
He'll put an apple in your lying mouth
And cook you in a sulfur stew,
One that will never be through
Is it soup yet? No!

Oh, if Jesus hadn't rescued me
Then I'd be down there cooking too.
Oh, if Jesus hadn't rescued me
Then I'd be cooking right next to you. Oooh!

I used to lie awake at night
And see your face on the ceiling,
Ha, ha, what a great feeling I have

When I think of how
You're gonna get yours,
At the end of the world, at the end of the world,
Yes at the end of the world!

*Restore to me the joy of your salvation and grant me a
willing spirit, to sustain me. Then I will teach trans-
gressors your ways, and sinners will turn back to you.*
—PSALM 51:12,13

If I asked you to guess who was the hardest type of person to
reach for Christ—junkies, prisoners, or Bible-Belt churchgoers,
you'd probably never choose the Bible Belters. But I've done a
lot of traveling, I've given a lot of concerts, and it's been those
who have attended church all their lives that I've had the hardest time reaching.

Sometimes it almost seems like their faith is more a part of
their culture in the Bible Belt than a reflection of a changed
heart. They've been attending Sunday school since they were
brought home from the hospital. They've learned all the right
memory verses and can recite the books of the Bible in less than
ten seconds. They know John 3:16 like it's their family motto.
But in all this, they still don't seem to have any spiritual life.
They tell me they asked Jesus into their hearts, usually as a
small child, but when I talk about knowing Christ as their *living
Lord,* when I speak of a *relationship* with Christ, they look back
at me with blank faces. That's why they're so hard to reach. If a
person doesn't know by experience that he or she desperately
needs a Savior, an everyday Savior, not a once-a-week-on-Sunday
Savior—they won't come to Him.

A junkie or a prisoner or an alcoholic or any other kind of
sinner knows by experience that they need Jesus. Their corrupt
heart tells them so every day. Maybe I should say, *our* corrupt
hearts tell us so. Because I'm in the class of those who desperately
need Jesus. I hope you are too, because I've noticed one other
thing about Bible-Belt Christians: They don't all live in the

Bible Belt. These cultural Christians who have the trappings of the faith live in every nook and cranny of America. They come to my concerts and buy my records. But sadly, their religiosity keeps them away from Christ.

Today, set aside your cultural religion. Live in Jesus. Be desperate for Him—because that's the only way you'll ever find Him.

71   How Do You Value Yourself?

What is your life? It is even a vapor that appears for a little time and then vanishes away.

—JAMES 4:14 NKJV

Sometimes we think more of ourselves than we should. After all, we're just dust. We're made up of a certain amount of fundamental elements that any chemist can identify. Someday we're going to die and our bodies will turn to dust. James says our life is but a vapor, here today, gone tomorrow. We're like the grass, which shoots up, withers, and dies. We're so very, very mortal.

But sometimes we think less of ourselves than we should. Within this frame of dust we carry around with us, we sense that we're meant for greater things than the approaching grave. God has set eternity in our hearts, and like a tree bending to the light, we bend towards God, reaching, yearning.

When we're tempted to think so little of ourselves, just remember the value God has placed on us: We're worth the death of His Son. That's the highest ransom ever paid. Though we often think too highly or too lowly of ourselves, let's never forget what God's estimation of our value is.

Dust to Dust

Sometimes it's hard to see,
Sometimes it's hard to get through to me,
But I want to do all that You ask me to.

Help me to follow through,
Make every day a devotion to You,
'Cause it's dust to dust,
Until we learn how to trust.

Sometimes I wander away,
You know lost in the dark,

My faith starts to sway
I don't know what to do,
So I cry out to You.
And I reach out in the air,
And I call Your name
And You're always there,
And You send down Your light,
And You tell me, walk by faith not by sight,
And then You come shining down.

I'm putting Your armor on,
Finding myself so suddenly drawn,
Like a moth to a flame,
Whenever You call my name.
Help me to follow through,
Make every day a devotion to You,
'Cause it's dust to dust,
Until we learn how to trust.

Sometimes I wander away,
And I'm lost in the dark,
My faith starts to sway
I don't know what to do,
So I cry out to You.
And I reach out in the air,
And I call Your name
And You're always there,
And You send down Your light,
And You tell me, walk by faith not by sight,
And then You come shining down.

Sometimes it's hard to see,
You know, sometimes it's hard to get through to me,
Sometimes it's hard to see,
You know, sometimes it's hard to get through to me,
But it's dust to dust
Until we learn how to trust.
Until we learn how to trust.

72　　Is Anyone Laughing at You?

*Blessed are you when people insult you, persecute you
and falsely say all kinds of evil against you because of
me. Rejoice and be glad, because great is your reward
in heaven, for in the same way they persecuted the
prophets who were before you.*

—MATTHEW 5:11,12

Do you ever get laughed at for your faith? Ridiculed for believing in Jesus? Then congratulations, you're living the normal Christian life. To the world, Christianity is foolishness and Christians are fools. They look at our joy and figure we must be "on something" to be this happy.

"What's happening? What are you smoking to get this high?" they ask. "Where can I get some?" So I tell them, "Hey man, it's free. It's trusting in Jesus. All the joy you can handle is *for free!*"

But they'd rather hear me tell them that I feel good because I'm loaded on some kind of drug. They don't understand—they think it's foolish to expect to live happily through Jesus. So they say, "It's gotta be phony. They must be smoking Bibles or something. What do they put in those communion wafers nowadays anyway?"

So they laugh it off and move on to their next "trip." The thing is, when that happens, the words of Jesus are being fulfilled. He promised that Christians would face persecution for His sake. We should expect to be laughed at and we should remember that we're in good company—He was laughed at too, and down through history, His most useful servants were all laughed at. That doesn't mean that we should all go out of our way to be laugh-at-able, but that we should expect it when it comes. Not just expect it—even better—we should *welcome* it because part of the promise of being laughed at is also the conveying of a *blessing*. But just remember that Jesus didn't say, "Blessed are you when you're obnoxious for the Lord." Let's make sure the laughter isn't deserved because of some fleshly foolishness on our part.

If your faith is real and you're ridiculed, then you must count it as joy. And consider the blessedness of being ridiculed for Jesus.

...Jesus Christ, who is Lord of all.

—ACTS 10:36

Dare to believe in Jesus. So many people are afraid because all they've seen of Jesus is "churchianity." They're turned off by the hypocrisy, but in spite of the presence of hypocrites in the church, there is a real Jesus and there are real Christians running around. The word *Christian* means "little Christ" and the implication is that each of us is supposed to be like a little Jesus running around doing what He did. Loving like He did.

Dare to reach out to others. Dare to believe in the power of Jesus to take care of your problems, your illnesses, your depressions, your relationships—whatever you need. We all have problems. Nobody gets off the planet without having some worries, trials, and griefs. But Jesus offers us rest in the midst of every sorrow and situation. No sin is too big, no problem too small for Him.

Dare to worship Him.

Jesus Is Lord of All!

Jesus is Lord of all
Jesus is Lord of all
No sin is too big
No problem too small,
Jesus is Lord of all.

Jesus is King of Kings
My Lord is King of Kings,
Presidents, princes, paupers will sing,
Jesus is King of Kings.

Jesus Christ is Lord of all,
King of Kings and Lord of Lords.
Ya know He's Lord of all.

Jesus is coming soon
Jesus is coming soon!
Just look in your heart
And see if there's room.
Jesus is coming soon.

Jesus Christ is Lord of all. Yes, yes, yes!
King of Kings and Lord of Lords.
That's all there is, that's all.

My God is Lord of all.
Jesus is Lord of all
No sin is too big
No problem too small,
Jesus is Lord of all.

*I do not ask Thee to take them out of the world, but to
keep them from the evil one. They are not of the
world, even as I am not of the world.*

—JOHN 17:15,16 NASB

In these last days, God is calling us to be in, but not part of, the
world. Too often we've grieved God by calling ourselves
Christians and then living like the world. To be a Christian is to
be different. But we want to have our faith and the lures of the
world too. And that's what they are—lures. Just like a fisherman
finds the glittery bait by which to hook his prey, so too has Satan,
the god of this world, baited his hook for believers. He knows if
we will accept Christ but still draw our nourishment from the
attractions of the world, he can render us ineffective as
Christians. Our prayers are short-circuited, our testimony is
diluted, and our world-fed flesh rules us.

The call from God is to repent. Turn our hearts away from the
world and give them wholly to Jesus. In our repentance it
wouldn't hurt if we could weep before the Lord with tears flowing from a genuinely broken heart. Such tears are cleansing to
the soul, when they're real.

The call is not to go live in a cave somewhere or to put on
camel-hair robes and eat locusts. The call is toward our heart. Will
we obey God and separate ourselves to be used for His purposes?

As we approach the final day, the enemy's lures may seem
more enticing, the pull on our flesh may seem irresistible, but
when Satan comes in like a flood, God raises His banner and
offers strength to stand firm.

Not everyone will be part of the remnant. But some will. May
you be part of that remnant army still on the battlefield when He
returns.

Here I am! I stand at the door and knock. If anyone hears my voice and opens the door, I will come in and eat with him, and he with me.

—REVELATION 3:20

Some people think that to be a proper Christian you have to speak in a James Mason English accent. That if someone looks into your eyes, they should see stained glass windows. That a good Christian always looks good, smells good, and has every hair in place.

Well, that lets me out. It lets out Jesus too—and just about all of us. The real test of a Christian is a changed heart. A Christian is someone who has traded his old corrupt heart for a new heart. And the way to do that is to let Jesus in when He comes knocking at your door. He approaches all of us and gently knocks, asking if we'd care to have fellowship with Him. To *dine* with Him. Think about how pleasant it is to have conversation and fellowship over dinner with someone who loves you. It's a time to share the kind of day you've had, what you'd like to do with your life, what worries you—stuff like that. Dinner is a time for talking. In the days when Jesus walked the earth, to eat with someone was a sign of approval and intimacy.

Have you ever been to a popular restaurant at dinnertime? Can you imagine if they had a sign posted that said, "No talking during dinner!"

In this verse Jesus was giving us a picture of what He wants of us—our most intimate fellowship. It doesn't mean that He wants to open a restaurant in our hearts. It means He wants to talk to us and to listen to us, *intimately*.

Too often we get Christianity all wrong. Jesus came to earth to *love us*. He didn't come to stomp on our heads or to judge us. He came here to save us. To put His arms around us. His mercy triumphs over judgment and this mercy is that which comes from the Father. In Jesus, God displays the depth of His mercy toward His people.

Today we have a dinner date with Jesus. He knocks even now, telling us that it's time to eat a meal with Him. Enjoy your fellowship with Jesus. He enjoys His fellowship with you.

76 It's Either You or the Rocks

I tell you...if they keep quiet, the stones will cry out.

—LUKE 19:40

Before I was a Christian, I was pretty skeptical about Christians. Frankly, they bugged me. Always going around saying "praise the Lord!"

Even when I got saved, I vowed I'd never say "praise the Lord." I thought to myself, *Okay, I'll sing a hymn now and then—maybe even something like "Onward Christian Soldiers"—and I'll read the Bible, but you'll never catch me saying anything as religious and trite as "praise the Lord."*

And one day I was writing in my diary and I got to the end of what I wanted to say and I closed with, "God is so good. Praise the Lord!" And all of a sudden I blurted out, "Oh no! I wrote 'Praise the Lord.'"

The next day Melody came up to me and said, "Keith, I just started to say, 'Praise the Lord.' I said, 'Praise...' and I caught myself. What am I gonna do?"

What else could we do? I said, "Melody, we're gonna have to give up. There's no use in fighting it. It's the Spirit of God... *Praise the Lord.*" And from then on we didn't fight it. And look what happened.

Face it, when you love the Lord, your mouth is gonna speak it. Don't fight it. Let it begin in your heart and work its way up through your pipes and come out your mouth.

Just praise the Lord. If you don't, the rocks will.

I am the true vine, and my Father is the gardener. He cuts off every branch in me that bears no fruit, while every branch that does bear fruit he prunes so that it will be even more fruitful.

—JOHN 15:1,2

God looks for fruit among His people. Without fruit, we're worthless as Christians. And God is constantly working with us and through us to make us more fruitful. If He sees that by pruning us we'll bear more fruit, then He prunes us. If we need watering, He'll send the rain. If we need some sunshine, He brings the light to shine on us. And if He sees that our roots are threatened by the many weeds around us, He'll start to cut away the weeds.

Sometimes we don't like that. We think, *No, Lord, don't cut away that weed—it's my favorite little weed. Why not let it stay? It doesn't sap away too much of my strength.* Yes, we've all got our favorite little weeds, and when God pulls them out by the roots, it can hurt. But it must be done.

God's got a goal for His people—a goal of fruitfulness. Look at your life. What are the weeds that are sprouting up around you? What little dandelions are distracting you from your calling? Will you invite God to yank them out?

Today, identify them by saying them out loud, and as you do, give them over to God.

There remains a Sabbath rest for the people of God. For the one who has entered His rest has himself also rested from his works, as God did from His.

—HEBREWS 4:9,10 NASB

God is making of us a new race of people. Not a race identified by nationality or some other outward characteristic, but a new nation comprised of black, white, yellow, red, green, purple, chartreuse, or whatever color you can think of. This nation isn't of the earth, but is a heavenly nation, and the inhabitants now walk on this earth in search of a kingdom.

Like the children of Israel walked through the desert looking for their promised land, so we too are pilgrims and strangers walking on a temporary earth. The Christian who puts down roots in this world is like a traitor. He has stopped the journey and decided to settle down in the desert. What a foolish mistake! To give up a land of plenty, designed to meet our every need, for the empty glitz of *earth*.

The land to which we're traveling (and which gets closer to us every day) is the land where we have a mansion built especially for us. Our own home. Comfortable, secure, and perfect in every way. In this new kingdom, we will dwell forever with Jesus our Lord. This land is a land of rest. No striving, no stress, no depression, no struggle—only rest. And while we move toward that land, we may enter that rest *now*.

No Christian should struggle when God has invited him to rest *now*. Just like eternal life isn't something we inherit when we die, it's something we possess now, so too is God's rest.

If you've never accepted God's rest for you as a Christian, don't wait any longer. Enter into that rest now. It'll make the rest of your earthly journey so much better.

Yet, O LORD, you are our Father. We are the clay,
you are the potter; we are all the work of your hand.
—ISAIAH 64:8

God wants us to be big in Him and small in ourselves. We must decrease so that He may increase. The way for that to happen is for us to confess, "God, I'm only dust, but make me into a jewel for You." Like a diamond, maybe? But we forget diamonds were once chunks of coal that had to undergo tons of pressure for a very long time until they were finally formed into rare and beautiful diamonds.

In the book of Isaiah, the image of a pot is used to describe the process God uses to mold us. Right now most of us are like those earthenware pots from Mexico with little donkeys painted on them. You put water in them, and they crumble. They're just adobe—dust formed into the shape of a pot.

But God wants fine china for His house. Vessels for His use. The way that happens is for our adobe pots to be put in the fiery kiln of affliction. Another word for affliction is "trial." That's where we really learn how to live life—in the furnace of trials. That's where the clay is hardened into a useful vessel; that's where the dross is refined out of the valuable ore.

If you ever hear someone say, "I'm a Christian and I never go through trials," then you'd better think about witnessing to that person, because their salvation is doubtful. You can't be a Christian without trials. That's like saying you can be a useful pot without going through the kiln or you can become a diamond without going through the process that turns coal into diamonds.

Never resent your trials. They are God's kiln designed for you. And every Christian has different trials. God has engineered for every one of us the specific kinds of trials that will work best to make us vessels of honor.

Embrace your trial; don't run from it. By embracing it, you embrace God's plan for you and you receive His grace in your affliction.

*Godliness with contentment is great gain. For we
brought nothing into the world, and we can take nothing out of it.*

—1 TIMOTHY 6:6,7

We came into this world alone, and we're going to leave it
alone. We can't take anyone or anything with us. Knowing this,
we should always be careful about claiming ownership over
material goods and, even more, other people. We must let all our
possessions be as though we don't really possess them. Even with
our children, we must let them be God's children, not *our* children. We don't own them—and it's as we surrender them to God
that we can really enjoy them as gifts God has entrusted to us as
stewards.

Give your children over to God, and they will become your
true children. Give your wife or husband over to God, and he or
she will be a true wife or husband. If you have many friends, give
them all to God, and they will become true friends.

Give everything you have to God. Let Him sanctify that
which He has given you, and all your worldly goods will be God's
possessions that He entrusted to you as a caretaker. That's all you
can do anyway.

Even this earthly frame we inhabit isn't ours really. We only
rent our bodies for about 80 years, and then God calls us home
and we receive our spiritual body. There's nothing on earth that
we really can claim as our own. And if we really want God's best
for us, we will cease to hunger after earthly possessions. There's
nothing here that will satisfy.

What is there in your life that's hard to surrender to God? We
all have family and friends, our pet longings, our favorite toys

that we don't want to give up. We're like children in a playpen hanging on desperately to our stuffed doggy while our daddy is waiting to give us a real, live puppy, if we'll only let go.

Offer everyone and everything up to God today. All of it.

81

If any man sin, we have an advocate with the Father,
Jesus Christ the righteous.

—1 JOHN 2:1 KJV

Think about your first day in heaven. You're waiting in line with a bunch of other people to see if you're going to get in. The guy ahead of you has a list in his hand, and as he's summoned before God, the thunderous voice of the Father asks him, "What did you do with Jesus?"

He looks at his list and answers, "Well, uh, I did lots of good stuff on earth. I gave to charity, I helped little old ladies across the street, I always said 'God bless you' when someone sneezed, and during all those years of Sunday school, I never stuck my gum under the desk."

But again God asks, "What did you do about Jesus?"

"Er…I read my Bible every so often. I really loved the twenty-third psalm. Especially that part about the green pastures."

"But what about Jesus? Did you love Him?"

"Uh, well, I thought He was a really good man. Wasn't that enough? I mean, after all, I did lots of Christian things in my life."

So God says, "Hmm. Let me ask My Son." So Jesus walks over and looks at the guy and says, "Who are you? I've never known you."

And that's that.

Now it's your turn. You walk up to God without a list in your hand. You're so awed by heaven you can't help but go, "Wow! This is *fantastic!* It's just like I thought it would be. And there's God! Hi, Daddy!"

God looks at you with a big smile and tears of joy running down His cheeks. The angels are exclaiming, "That one is one of His! I recognize him!"

But just then the devil walks in and *he's* got a list. You look at him and say, "Uh-oh. I didn't know it was going to be like this."

So Satan starts reading off the list. He mentions that summer day in August 1974 when you lusted after that cheerleader. And then he brings up that episode with the LSD and the marijuana. He seems to really delight in telling about that pornographic movie you watched at that bachelor party in June of 1979. He goes on and on about how judgmental you were and the times you failed to be the perfect little Christian. Finally he concludes with that time just before you died when you got angry at the guy who cut you off in traffic.

Right about then your palms are sweating. You suddenly feel warmer and wonder if that's because you're ready to be cast away into the fiery inferno. Just then God says, "Okay, let's hear from the counsel for the defense."

So Jesus walks up and says, "Hey Dad, this one's Mine."

That's all it takes for God to hammer His gavel and say, "Case dismissed!"

Brothers, sisters…we have an advocate with the Father. Our case before God is dismissed. *Forever.*

Rest in assurance today that Satan's case against you can't triumph over the power of the blood Jesus shed for you. Rejoice in your *Savior.* He rejoices in you.

82

Unexpected Ministry Opportunities

Cast all your anxiety on him because he cares for you.
—1 PETER 5:7

Catalina High School, Tucson, Arizona

We have a new motor home in which we travel to our concert dates. We bought it two months ago so our family of eight Christians old and new in Jesus could grow closer together. For the first three or four weeks, while we were still at home, we had the motor home in the shop, trying to get all the bugs worked out of it. But all the bugs wouldn't leave. We even tried Raid! But things kept going wrong—like the day the water tank burst and all of a sudden we had an indoor swimming pool, which wasn't too good on the rugs.

It never did get fixed right. Yesterday the water line broke again for the tenth time and went back for yet another repair. Then this morning the generator blew up and now we find that the refrigerator isn't working. So with this Arizona heat, we have hot food in our refrigerator. I told Melody that if I weren't a Christian, I'd be having ulcers and heart attacks over all this stuff. But because I *am* a Christian, I know that God's in control. I guess He wants us to have a ministry to mechanics. In L.A. one of the guys working on the RV came over for dinner. That night there were about 12 of us at dinner and this guy, Bernie, couldn't get over our unity. Yesterday we got to witness to another mechanic in Phoenix. The Lord must really love RV mechanics is all I can say.

Anyway, as we sat around in the waiting room for them to work on the thing, I said, "We really need to pray for a miracle. This is a $2,000 generator. It operates the whole electrical system of our ark." (We call our RV the "ark" and right now it's not floating too well. The animals are running around out of their cages.) But what happened was that we tried to call the factory in Minneapolis to see if they would authorize just trading a brand-new generator for the broken one. I was told that if I would tell the guy we'd only used the generator for about 10 hours, they might do it. But I knew we'd used it for at least 25 hours, and I wouldn't lie about it. He said, "There's a difference between a fib and lie." I had to tell him, "Not to Jesus there isn't."

I'd like to say that my truthfulness paid off. But in the natural it didn't. Now we have to drive from here to Dallas to get it fixed. Five days in the hot summer sun without air conditioning. You've heard of "Shake 'n' Bake"? Well, we're gonna be "drive 'n' bake." But I have one more opportunity. I have to call the factory again tomorrow, and apparently if I can come up with a convincing reason for them to replace the generator, they still might do it. But I won't lie.

In the midst of all this mania, we've been having so much fun in Jesus. I can't believe so many good things could come out of so many trials, but that's the way God works. I've come to rest in this. There's nothing to worry about. This is His tour and His vehicle. These are His RV mechanics with whom we're having divine appointments. And what a way to witness. The mechanics in L.A. couldn't believe that I'd come back with the same problem for the tenth time and not cuss at them. Usually they're having fistfights with people on the tenth visit, but I figured out something real spiritual a long time ago: *Worrying about the situation doesn't change anything.*

Every trial has its place in the plan of God. Instead of worry or anxiety, look for God's opportunity for ministry in the situation. Rejoice in what God's doing *all the time*, but especially when you can't understand what He's doing.

The wisdom of this world is foolishness before God.
—1 CORINTHIANS 3:19 NASB

Yesterday as we sat in the waiting room while our RV was being worked on, we witnessed to a Jewish guy and his wife who were also waiting. Since I'm Jewish I had a lot to say. His response was, "I read *The Passover Plot,* and it disproves all that stuff you believe, doesn't it?" I told him it proves that a lot of people can get rich by writing books that try to discredit God. Then I said something that was kind of surprising, but from the Lord. I told him, "Your intellect is going to kill you. Your reasoning is going to suffocate the life out of any hope you have of getting to heaven."

I sensed that if he had left the room, his wife might pray with us. The look in her eyes was, "I want it. I want it. But I can't. I can't." It was like "We're atheists together. We don't believe in God, do we, honey?" It was so sad. Someday she'll stand before the Lord and He'll ask, "Why didn't you ask Me into your heart that day that Keith witnessed to you?" She'll respond, "Because of my husband. He was responsible." But that won't work with God. We all stand before God alone.

We all must decide now, on our own. And if our intellect is what drives us, we'll miss heaven. Jesus said we must become as little children to inherit the kingdom. How intellectual are kids? They're so innocent that they can believe without being worried about being embarrassed. Embarrassment is just an indicator of pride at work.

Don't let your intellect be the death of you. Don't let your pride determine your future—both now and for all eternity. Be simple. Be humble. Be a child.

Give ear to my words, O LORD,
Consider my meditation.
Hearken unto the voice of my cry, my King,
And my God:
For unto thee will I pray.
My voice shalt thou hear in the morning,
O LORD; in the morning
Will I direct my prayer
Unto thee, and will look up.

—PSALM 5:1-3 KJV

The brother who wrote the music to the worship chorus of Psalm 5 was a man named Bill Sprouse. I never met him, but I feel close to him. Many of my friends knew him, and they've told me about him.

Bill was lead singer and keyboard player for a group called "The Road Home." He died of a heart attack just a month after he wrote this chorus. In fact, the song is recorded on the *Maranatha 5* album, and Bill laid down the tracks for that recording and died the next day. This was his last gift to the church and his most beautiful.

That which we are working on today may seem trivial—simply a matter of course. We do what we're given to do and move on, day by day, never really thinking about the work we will one day leave behind. Our calling may be music or it may be scrubbing toilets for the Lord, but whatever it is, we should make it the best…just in case it's the last gift we leave behind.

The reason my Father loves me is that I lay down my life—only to take it up again. No one takes it from me, but I lay it down of my own accord.

—JOHN 10:17,18

We forget what it must have been like on the cross. We forget the pain that Jesus suffered. Besides the horrible physical pain, there was the worse pain of being separated from the Father. It says that Jesus *became sin* on the cross for us. He became our sin. Let that sink in a minute. All that sin that's running through your veins right now, He became *that*. And then when He was nailed to the cross, our sin was put to death on the cross with Him. What do you think that was like for Jesus?

We know that He cried out, "God, why have you forsaken me?" in great anguish. He felt what it was like to be separated from God and it freaked Him out. And then we hear Him declare, "It is finished." He had accomplished what God sent Him to do—but at an unspeakable cost.

When we see the crucifixion on TV or in a movie, it's always the same, they show the whole scene in about 45 seconds. But in real time, it was hours and hours Jesus hung on the cross, the large spikes through His hands and feet, the crown of thorns on His head. But even with all that pain, Jesus didn't die of blood loss. He died of a broken heart. It says that when they pierced His side, water and blood came out. There's a little sac around the human heart called the pericardium that on very rare occasions, under tremendous pressure, can burst. The blood veins can start to burst inside you also under this kind of stress. And we know too that the night before the crucifixion, when Jesus prayed about a Plan B, He sweated drops of blood. The blood vessels in His forehead broke and mixed with sweat—that's how intense the stress was. He was fully human and fully God at the same time. And during this awful time, we see the humanity of Jesus.

Just imagine. That prayer in Gethsemane was probably something like, "Father, I've lived with You in heaven since eternity past. We've seen people die for centuries. But now I've got to die too. And even worse, I've got to be separated from You. Father, I don't know if I can go through with this. Isn't there anything else that can be done? *Anything?* I know You said that there's no forgiveness without the shedding of blood, but can't We come up with a new plan?"

Jesus wanted to avoid the cross—if there was another way. But there wasn't. And obedience to God was more important than avoiding pain to Jesus. So He gave His life. Nobody killed Jesus. No one *took* His life. He said that all He had to do was summon angels and they would get Him down off the cross. And after all, Jesus had turned water to wine, healed desperately sick people, raised the dead, and walked on water—do we really think that He couldn't get himself down off the cross to save His life if He thought there were another way? No, Jesus went willingly to the cross and sacrificed His life—it wasn't taken from Him.

Bow low before Him today. Bow before the One who took your place on the cross and became your sin so you could become the righteousness of God in Him.

Hallelujah! He is worthy!

*You also must be ready, because the Son of Man will
come at an hour when you do not expect him.*
—MATTHEW 24:44

We have many choices to make in life. But if we say, "I'll wait
until my deathbed and then I'll get right with God," we're being
foolish. He might not call us on that day. You don't have a choice
as to when you can come. You only have a choice to come *when
He calls*. But today He is calling us, wooing us, inviting us…if
we'll open up to Him. But if He's not calling, you can't go.

Consider the parable of the ten virgins. It was a Saturday
night and all ten of them were getting ready for the nice Jewish
wedding. It was about 9:30 and off to a slow start—Jewish
weddings can be that way. By about 10:30 the girls had dozed off.
But then at midnight a trumpet sounded announcing the immi-
nent arrival of the bridegroom. They all awoke and trimmed
their lamps. But only five of the virgins had been wise enough to
plan ahead and bring extra oil.

The other five were frantic about getting more oil. They
started begging the prepared virgins for help. "Hey Shirley, can I
borrow some of your oil?" or "Please, Ethel, you know I always
liked you. Give me some of your oil." But the wise virgins only
had enough for their own lamps. Shirley said, "Hey girls, there's
an all-night Shell station down the road about a mile, why don't
you go buy some more?" So the five foolish virgins scurried off.
As they left, they called back, "Wait for us! We'll be right back!"
And off they went.

Meanwhile the bridegroom arrives and says, "I thought there
were ten of you. What happened to the other five? You mean
they went out at this hour to buy oil? Well, I'll deal with that

later." So he invites the wise virgins into the wedding supper and bolts the door behind them. An hour later, the foolish virgins come riding up. "Wow, look," they say. "There's a party going on inside. Maybe we can get dessert." So they knock on the door. "Let us in!" they cry. "We have our oil now. Let us in!"

The butler comes to the door and says, "What do you want? We're having a party. Go away."

"No," they cry. "We want to talk to the bridegroom!"

The butler sighs. "Just a minute. I'll ask."

Soon the bridegroom peers out the window and asks, "Who are you girls, anyway? I don't know you."

The virgins are thus turned away at the door, all as a result of their foolishness—of not being *ready*. You ask, how can my loving God do that? It's because He's tired of pew-warming Christians who are asleep through life. They act religious, they donate to the stained glass fund, and they are pretty nice people. But they're nice people whose lamps are low on oil, with none to spare.

In the Bible, oil represents the Holy Spirit. If you don't have the oil of the Holy Spirit, how do you belong to Him? This Holy Spirit oil is the oil of gladness, of joy, of peace. If we're like the wise virgins, we'll be sure to have plenty of oil to last until the Bridegroom comes. We'll walk full of the Holy Spirit of God 24 hours a day.

I, if I am lifted up from the earth, will draw all men to Myself.

—JOHN 12:32 NASB

Sometimes people come up to the front of the stage and take pictures of me. Others ask for my autograph. But it's Jesus whose image we need burned into our hearts. We need to be asking the Lord to write His name on our hearts.

Sometimes I reluctantly sign an autograph. It's easier than explaining why I hate to do it. What I really want to tell them is that it's my goal to leave as little of me on the earth as possible. It's Jesus who I want to point people towards, not Keith Green.

I don't want someone to wake up in the morning and say, "I wanna hear Keith Green." I'd much rather they say, "I wanna hear from Jesus."

Sometimes when I come onstage I hear screams and shouts of happiness that I never hear directed towards Jesus, the only One who brings happiness. I go into the music department of Christian bookstores, and I see all these posters with Christian musicians, but I don't see a poster of Jesus.

We don't need to copy the world and have a host of Christian celebrities. In fact, in God's eyes there are no Christian celebrities. There's just Jesus. And if just Jesus isn't enough for you, then buying posters won't help you one bit.

Follow only Jesus and those who are following Him.

Do not merely listen to the word, and so deceive your-selves. Do what it says. Anyone who listens to the word but does not do what it says is like a man who looks at his face in a mirror and, after looking at himself, goes away and immediately forgets what he looks like. But the man who looks intently into the perfect law that gives freedom, and continues to do this, not forgetting what he has heard, but doing it— he will be blessed in what he does.

—JAMES 1:22-25

Jesus Festival, 1978

I bet that right about now, those of you who have been here for three days are at your saturation point. You've heard a lot of teaching, lots of singing, and lots of praising. A lot of hot dogs, hoagies, and ice cream have passed your lips. Right about now, you just wanna go home. You're tired of the mud, you're tired of being around 20,000 other people, and all you want is a shower and your own bed.

But, bless you, you've stayed to hear Keith Green bring the festival to a close. You might be expecting some big emotional, incredible, mind-blowing finale. But my job in closing is to make sure that you go home and do what you were told here. Well, of course, that's really the Holy Spirit's job, but this is what I've felt impressed by God to share with you—obedience to the things you've heard.

At a big party like this, everybody gets all riled up. You're feeling good. You've resolved to go home and make some big changes in your life. People at church will ask you about Jesus '78 and you'll say, "Man, you shoulda been there! It was just so incredible!" And then the following week you'll say, "Yeah, it was really pretty neat. I mean wait a second, I'll go back and check my notes." The next week, someone will say, "Are you sure you were really there? I can't tell—your life is back to where it was three weeks ago." And they'll be right.

How come when we hear an incredible speaker and great music, we go home all fired up, only to lose our passion within a couple of weeks? It's because, in the words of James, we've not become doers of the Word. We've become hearers only, deceiving ourselves.

Brothers, *doing the Word perpetuates the Word*. The more you do of what you've heard, empowered by God, the more He gives you to do. If you don't do what you're told, you'll stop being told. And if you don't listen with your heart and put it into action, it becomes loss to you. There's nothing worse than praise and worship that's not followed by obedience. It's hollow.

It doesn't have to be that way. Let the words you've heard become meat to you in the days ahead. Keep going with God. Keep believing, and let your believing propel you to action. That's the way to get the blessing you seek.

*Has the LORD as much delight in burnt offerings and
sacrifices as in obeying the voice of the LORD? Behold,
to obey is better than sacrifice, and to heed than the fat
of rams.*

—1 SAMUEL 15:22 NASB

As I travel around the country I see a lot of good ministries for
the Lord—and some that aren't so good. I meet a lot of
Christians who seem zealous—and some who seem lifeless. I've
met fundamentalists, charismatics, Lutherans, Episcopalians, and
just about every other brand of Christian you can think of. And
some of them were real brothers and sisters in the Lord. Others
just seemed to know a lot about religion. Then I come home and
get into my Bible and find myself asking, "God, with all this
activity going on in Your name, why isn't more happening? Why
aren't we experiencing revival?"

When I was first baptized in the Spirit, I thought the answer
was just getting more people baptized in the Spirit. But then I
saw that many who were baptized in the Spirit weren't living
lives much different from anyone else. I heard people speaking in
tongues, casting out demons, and healing the sick, but in their
private life, they were struggling just like everyone else.

Then I'd visit some huge churches where they had a fantastic
minister and all sorts of dynamic programs. I'd attend worship
services and see people jumping up and down in the name of the
Lord, shouting and having a great time. But I'd watch the people
after the service and see that they weren't any different from
other Christians. Where was the *agape* love, the unity, the
revival God wants? I just couldn't figure it out.

"God, what is it?" I asked. "What are we missing?" And the Lord kept bringing me back time and again to obedience. To obey is better than any sacrifice we can give. Where I used to think that the baptism with the Spirit was the end-all for the Christian, I began to see that the real answer is daily *walking in the Spirit.* Anyone can have an "experience" that gives them momentary goose bumps. But goose bumps go away. The fruit of obedience *lasts.*

To Obey Is Better Than Sacrifce

To obey is better than sacrifice,
I don't need your money, I want your life.
And I hear you say that I'm coming back soon,
But you act like I'll never return.
Well you speak of grace and My love so sweet,
How you thrive on milk, but reject My meat,
And I can't help weeping of how it will be,
If you keep on ignoring My words.
Well you pray to prosper and succeed,
But your flesh is something I just can't feed.
To obey is better than sacrifice.
I want more than Sunday and Wednesday nights,
'Cause if you can't come to Me every day,
Then don't bother coming at all.
La, la, la...
To obey is better than sacrifice.
I want hearts of fire, not your prayers of ice.
And I'm coming quickly, to give back to you,
According to what you have done,
According to what you have done,
According to what you have done.

*Seeing a lone fig tree by the road, He came to it and
found nothing on it except leaves only; and He said to
it, "No longer shall there ever be any fruit from you."
And at once the fig tree withered.*

—MATTHEW 21:19 NASB

A fig tree doesn't become a fig tree by making figs. A fig tree is
born because God sent a bee along to pollinate the blossom of
another fig tree. The blossom turns into a fig with fig seeds in it.
The fig then falls to the ground and rots. The fig seeds germinate
and up comes a fig tree.

The fig tree that Jesus approached was a fig tree by a gift of
God expressed through nature. It didn't *do* anything to become a
fig tree. It just stood there being a fig tree, thinking to itself,
"Here I am being a fig tree." And God came up to this fig tree in
the form of Jesus and said, "I'm hungry. Give me some figs. Let
me see your fruit."

The fig tree was silent. Fig trees do that sometimes. Jesus
said, "C'mon...a Fig Newton...anything." The fig tree remained
silent.

So Jesus cursed the fig tree for not bearing fruit and the tree
withered and died. The fig tree didn't have to make figs to be a
fig tree—it already was a fig tree by the life that was in it. It
couldn't be anything other than a fig tree—like a redwood tree
or a pine tree. But because it was a fig tree, it should bear the fruit
of a fig tree. It should give out nourishment. It should reproduce.
But to just stand there in silence rejoicing in its heritage as a fruit
tree is foolishness.

What is our identity? Isn't it that of a Christian? The life of
God has been reproduced in us for a reason. God comes along

and rightfully expects to see the fruit of the life we have within us. If there's no life there, of what use are we?

The life of Jesus in us wants to work itself out in the form of serving others, ministering, feeding, nourishing those whom God has given us. He also has the expectation that the life within us will reproduce itself in others.

Be fruitful and multiply. Replenish the kingdom of God with figs...er, new believers.

...remembering the words the Lord Jesus himself said:
"It is more blessed to give than to receive."

—ACTS 20:35

Brothers, sisters, we're so wealthy with this world's riches. What a responsibility we have. The world is full of dying, starving people, and we have more than we need every single day. And what do we do with what we have? At a minimum we might send off our $20 a month to World Vision to support an orphan. We say, "Yeah, I've got a child I support in Outer Mongolia. I'm doin' my part for sure." We take pride in the fact that we do without a Snickers bar every so often in the name of Christ, so we can feed our orphan. We sigh that we won't be able to get the tinted windshield on our new Mercedes. Life is so tough.

And then we hear teaching from some Christians that God's prosperity is what we should be seeking. God wants us to be rich. Get that tinted windshield after all. God would want it that way. But then these teachers tell us how to get this prosperity—we must give first. "If you want to get, you've got to give," they say. "Keep on giving so you can keep on getting."

What an ugly reason for a Christian to be giving. Just so he can *get* something. Did Jesus give His life for us just so He could get a bunch of people? *No! He gave His life because He loved us!*

Is it possible that we can give out of the same motivation as Jesus—with no thought of getting anything back? Can we give without calculating every penny? What if we told our spouse, "Well, I'll give myself to you on Tuesdays, Thursdays, and Saturdays. The rest of the time, I'm going to enjoy myself." The result would be a pretty poor excuse for a marriage. And to live for ourselves after claiming Jesus as our Lord makes for a poor excuse for being called a Christian.

Unless we use what we've got to glorify God—all of what we've got—we're just talking jive. And jive is the content of our Christianity. Here's a question for you: Have you spent more money in your Christian life on CDs, books, concerts, movies, posters—or on the poor?

What are you going to do about it?

Proclaim his salvation day after day. Declare his glory among the nations, his marvelous deeds among all peoples.

—PSALM 96:2,3

Christians are so busy wanting to be happy that they forget about being holy. Instead of fishing for men, preachers are more often fishing for compliments. "Did you like my sermon? Wasn't it good? Praise Gawd!"

But, folks, if we want to change the world, we're going to have to stop acting like other Christians and start acting like Jesus. That's such a simple truth, but really it's life-changing, if we'll do it. Instead of looking around at others and saying, "Well, they're not praying very much, why should I?" or "They aren't telling many people about Jesus, so I don't need to either," we should turn our eyes on Jesus.

Do we need to worry about what our neighbor is doing when we already know Jesus is telling us to "go into all the world and preach the gospel to every creature"? Jesus also said, "What I tell you in secret, proclaim from the housetops."

Too many of us are like secret agents for God. Silent witnesses. What an oxymoron that is. How can you be a silent witness for God? It's like Fred calls and you say, "Hey Fred, how'd you like the game yesterday? Huh? Oh sure, I can come over for a few beers and watch Monday night football at your place. I'll be there by 6:00." All the while we tell ourselves we're being a silent witness to Fred. Right.

Or how about this? Betty Lou calls and suggests going out for dinner and movie on Wednesday night. Of course that's the night of the prayer meeting, but, hey—here's a chance to witness to Betty Lou, so you say, "Sure." Maybe during the previews of coming attractions you can whip out your Bible and lead her to the Lord real fast.

"Ashamed of Jesus? Whatever gave you that idea? I'm just being a silent witness. I'm letting my life speak for the Lord." Oh, and what exactly is your life saying?

I've met girls who believe in missionary dating and some guys who feel called to a ministry to blondes. "Man, I've got a burden for that girl. I'm gonna date her for the Lord."

We try so hard to manipulate God into doing what we want done. We want to have fun, and so God becomes the God of fun. Enjoy a relationship with God and keep the pleasures of the world too. In southern California we've created a virtual Christian Disneyland of fun.

So many of us want God to bless our idea of Him, rather than us changing our idea of Him into who He really is. We read the verse about becoming all things to all men and we foolishly interpret that as an excuse to be worldly to reach the world. We do need to reach the lost—but through being a light with our words, actions, and LOVE. Not by being worldly.

But God is not someone we can easily be ashamed of. He is not offering burdens for blondes or looking for conversions during the coming attractions.

He is Lord. He is *Lord*. And He has no silent witnesses.

Think about it.

93   Do We Really Want Revival?

This is love, that we walk according to His command-
ments. This is the commandment, just as you have
heard from the beginning, that you should walk in it.

—2 John 6 NASB

There was this evangelist in the nineteenth century named Charles Finney who led about 500,000 people to the Lord in his lifetime. This was before microphones or megachurches or tel-evangelism. All Finney had going for him was the power of God working through him.

Finney said that revival is nothing more and nothing less than a new beginning of obedience to God, starting in God's people. He believed that Christians are more at fault for not being revived than sinners are for not being saved. Judgment begins at the house of God.

Revival comes when we Christians get serious about obeying God. The Lord wants to shake up His people, big time—but will we let Him? We think that revival is going to disrupt our life—and it will. But we desperately *need* our lives disrupted, shaken up. If we're honest, we'll admit that we're living below the level of joy and abundance God has for us. Revival—personal revival—will bring that joy. But to have it, we must cut loose of the sin that so easily besets us.

Every day offers each of us a new beginning of obedience to God, empowered not by our fleshly attempts at obedience, but by His Spirit working in us to obey. Today offers that same opportunity, that same new beginning. Trust God to show you how to obey Him. Ask Him to work through you. Take His yoke. His burden of obedience is light, not troublesome. It may shake you up, but it will bring joy.

Suppose one of you wants to build a tower. Will he not first sit down and estimate the cost to see if he has enough money to complete it?...In the same way, any of you who does not give up everything he has cannot be my disciple.

—LUKE 14:28,33

The problem today is that we have this idea that Jesus is this pill we take to make everything all right. All our problems will vanish the minute we ask Christ into our life. That's what I thought at first. That's what I preached for a while.

I'd say, "All you gotta do is receive Jesus and all your worries will be over." I'd say, "Here, John, just say this sinner's prayer with me: 'Lord Jesus, come into my heart, forgive my sin, and give me eternal life. Amen.' Okay, John, now you're a Christian. Welcome to the family of God. Now all you gotta do is fill out this card with your name and address, and we'll send some literature to you. Here's a schedule of our church meetings; see you then. Oh, if you have any questions, give me a call."

So two days later the phone rings. "Oh, hi, John. How ya' doin'? What? Trials? Oh yeah, I forgot to mention there might be some trials. So what's the problem, Johnny?"

Johnny says, "Well, you see, I can't figure out which girlfriend to throw out of the house."

"Er...which girlfriend?"

"Yeah. Well, Shirley and me were makin' love last night... man, we were so stoned out. It was really cool, man. I felt the power of God and everything and..."

"Uh, Johnny...did you know that as a Christian you need to give up your drugs?"

"Well gee, Keith—you didn't tell me that. I figure if God doesn't want me to take drugs, He'll just take them away, you know, like supernaturally. But Keith, smoking dope isn't my problem. My problem is that one of these girls has to go, man. I mean one of them is closer to receiving the Lord than the other, and she's a better lover anyway, so I figure I'll keep her around."

"Johnny, wait a minute. You've got it all wrong. You can't be a Christian and fornicate."

"Forni—what? Hey Keith, I thought Jesus was going to give me joy and peace and all these other groovy things. You never said anything about my dope and my girls."

"Johnny, God *will* give you joy and peace, but you've got to give Him your life."

"Well, I did. But you mean He wants my sex and my dope too?"

"Johnny, I think we better get together and talk."

"No, Keith. If being a Christian means giving up dope and sex with my girlfriend, let's just forget it. I take back my prayer."

"Johnny, you can't take back your prayer."

"Well, I do anyway." Click.

"Johnny, Johnny, wait!"

Whoops, lost another one. We don't talk much today about counting the cost of becoming a believer. We try to lead people to the Lord (if we bother to witness at all—and most Christians don't) and just get them in quickly. We want to close the deal before they change their minds or before they find out the truth—that there *is* a cost to becoming a Christian. We've made salvation cheap. And while salvation is free—it's not cheap. He who *loses his life for My sake* will find it.

95   Sometimes the Truth Hurts

Rejoice, you heavens and you who dwell in them! But woe to the earth and the sea, because the devil has gone down to you! He is filled with fury, because he knows that his time is short.

—REVELATION 12:12

Let's say you live in an apartment building and all of a sudden in the middle of the night you hear screams from the apartment next door. You smell smoke and you realize that there's a fire in the building. You go out in the hall and see that the fire is starting to engulf your whole building. You realize that many tenants are probably still asleep, so you go up and down the halls banging on doors, trying to get people to wake up. You might even break down a door or two and burst into an apartment and help someone get out. You'd do anything to save them. Maybe even risk your own life. Most people would respond the same way because of a natural compassion we feel for those in danger.

But what about the supernatural compassion Christians should have for the lost? Do we have it? There are people around us every day who are sinking down into a hellfire that is far worse than any physical fire. A human being caught up in a fire will only burn once. But the fire of hell burns eternally.

Maybe the difference in our responses to physical fire and the fires of hell is that we can see physical fires now while the fires of hell aren't visible. But if we could for one minute hear the cries from hell, see the agony of the condemned, we'd freak out and try to find a way to rescue them. Satan, of course, knows this and he does his best to keep hell as invisible as possible. He doesn't want us to know the horror the lost endure in hell. As a result, we go around with our "hallelujah, everything is just fine" attitude while our friends inch closer to the brink of hell with each passing day.

The Bible teaches us that we're responsible for what we know. And we know that hell awaits for the lost. But we also know something else. We know that *no one has to go to hell*. There is a Savior—One who said He came into the world, not to judge it, but to *save* it.

I was thinking this three weeks ago and the Lord gave me a song about how we slumber while the apartment is burning, while there are people who need to be warned. If we believe the Bible, we must wake up and warn others of the fire they face.

Asleep in the Light

Do you see, do you see?
All the people sinking down,
Don't you care, don't you care?
Are you gonna let them drown?
How can you be so numb,
Not to care if they come?
You close your eyes
And pretend the job's done…

Oh bless me Lord, bless me Lord,
You know it's all I ever hear,
No one aches, no one hurts,
No one even sheds one tear,
But He cries, He weeps, He bleeds,
And He cares for your needs,
And you just lay back and keep soaking it in,
Oh, can't you see it's such sin?

'Cause He brings people to your door,
And you turn them away,
As you smile and say,
"God bless you, be at peace,"
And all heaven just weeps,
'Cause Jesus came to your door,

You've left Him out on the streets.
Open up, open up,
And give yourself away,
You see the need, you hear the cry,
So how can you delay?
God's calling and you're the one,
But like Jonah you run,
He's told you to speak,
But you keep holding it in.
Oh, can't you see it's such sin?

The world is sleeping in the dark
That the church can't fight,
'Cause it's asleep in the light,
How can you be so dead?
When you've been so well fed,
Jesus rose from the grave,
And you, you can't even get out of bed,
Oh, Jesus rose from the dead,
Come on, get out of your bed.

How can you be so numb?
Not to care if they come,
You close your eyes and pretend the job's done,
You close your eyes and pretend the job's done,
Don't close your eyes, don't pretend the job's done.
Come away, come away,
Come away with Me, My love,
Come away from this mess,
Come away with Me, My love.

We, who are many, are one body in Christ, and individually members one of another. Since we have gifts that differ according to the grace given to us, each of us is to exercise them accordingly.

—ROMANS 12:5,6 NASB

I've had people come up to me and say, "Keith, you've done so much for my walk with the Lord." I'd say, "But I haven't done anything." Folks, I can't change anyone's life. I'm like a pencil, that's all. When you've written a letter with a pencil and it turned out good, you don't look at the pencil and say, "Wow, great pencil." You put the pencil in the drawer and forget about it. How many times have you heard a beautiful song on the radio that prompted you to get down on your knees and kiss the speaker because of the music that came through it?

I'm blessed when God uses me, but I'm not the one who gets the credit. God alone is the one who does the beautiful stuff. Keith Green is your basic ugly-inside converted sinner. It's truly a miracle He even uses me as a pencil.

And you know what? We're all like that. We all have gifts and abilities that are given to us to point others to the Lord. But we can take no credit for those gifts—we didn't give ourselves those gifts.

No one is any more special than anyone else. We're all in this together.

Because of You

People smile at me and ask me what it is
That makes them want to be just like I am.
So I just point to You

And tell them, yes it's true
I'm no special one, I'm just one man.

It's because of You,
People smile at me
And they say, what a lucky guy!
It's because of You,
I can raise my hands and reply
And say I'm happy because of You.

Now people can't believe
That my life used to be
Something no one
Had any use for.
I'd stay at home each night
Never shine the light
And I thank You,
It will never be like before.

It's because of You
People point at me
And they say, "I like what that boy's got."
But because of You,
I confess I don't have a lot
But what I've got is because of You.

Now people smile at me and ask me what it is
That makes them want to be just like I am.
So I just point to You
And tell them, yes it's true
I'm no special one, I'm just one man.

It's because of You,
People smile at me
And they say, what a lucky guy!
It's because of You,
I can raise my hands to the sky
And say I'm only happy because of You.

God, who knows the heart, showed that he accepted them by giving the Holy Spirit to them, just as he did to us. He made no distinction between us and them, for he purified their hearts by faith.

—ACTS 15:8,9

Someone once brought their grandmother to a youth meeting I was doing. She was saying, "I don't bear witness to this. I mean, it's one thing to have the long-haired weirdos out in the audience, but up on the pulpit—no, I don't think so!"

But you know what? It isn't what you look like that makes you a Christian. It's who you know. You have to know Someone in high places. God is so good that He's able to use someone who looks like me.

Not long ago I was on *The 700 Club*. They usually have a bunch of little old ladies from one of the local churches manning the phones and sitting in the audience. So for this occasion, I felt like I should trim my beard. So I trimmed it quite a bit and went on the program. And then in the middle of the interview, the guy says, "I hear you trimmed your beard to come on the show." So I fessed up. "I didn't want to offend your audience, either here in the studio or who might be watching. Some of them believe you ought to be saved and shaved."

After the show, one of these little old ladies came up to me with tears in her eyes and said, "You know, whenever somebody who looked like you came on the TV I turned it off. Now, after hearing you, I'll never do that again because you really ministered to me."

Folks, that broke my heart. It reminded me that if we let the light of Jesus shine through us, it won't really matter what we look like on the outside. They'll see Jesus.

You know, Jesus walked around the hot desert in the middle of summer without the advantage of Ban or Right Guard. He probably sweated profusely. Jesus probably would not look very appealing in our culture today. We've mouthwashed, hair-sprayed, and breath-minted ourselves way out of proportion. Outward appearance is so highly regarded among us. But to the Lord, unless you're looking good inside with Jesus radiating out of you, you might as well be wearing a gunnysack.

We walk out of our houses having spent a lot of time in front of the mirror making sure we look okay. But how much time do we spend each morning in the mirror of God's Word, making sure our inner man is groomed for the day?

There is salvation in no one else; for there is no other name under heaven that has been given among men by which we must be saved.

—ACTS 4:12 NASB

When I witness to people, I often get the same response: "Hey man, I don't need to become a Christian. I'll worship God my own way." That was the attitude I used to have. I believed in God. I worshiped God in many different ways and under many other names—but never Jesus. I thought it didn't matter what we called Him. All the names were essentially the same, right? Oh man, I was so deceived.

I used to go out in the desert on peyote, looking for Don Juan out among the cactus. I used to chant. I meditated. I sat at the feet of all the grooviest gurus. I paid money for books, lectures, drugs, and I learned all the latest mantras.

All that time one thing was always the same: If you just read one more book…if you just try one more drug…if you just hear one more speaker…if you just try one more yoga position—then you'll find enlightenment. But I never did. There were times when I'd be cruising along on acid for eight hours and then I'd come down still hungering for truth. I had to go find my connection to get more drugs, hoping the stuff was good and that I wouldn't have a bad trip.

With Jesus there are no bad trips. Only one very good trip. It's not drug induced and it never ends. It is one long journey from earth to heaven with God Himself as our Guide. It is pure and amazing and holy. Just like He is. I am eternally grateful I found the truth. I may not do everything right, but I know I am on the right path, following the only leader in the universe worth following. I hope you are following Him too.

Hallelujah.

Permissions and Acknowledgments

Melody Green Goes Online

Taking the Ministry of Keith Green and Last Days Ministries Classics to a new generation.

WWW.KEITHGREEN.COM OR WWW.MELODYGREEN.COM

Our Web site is a whole ministry in itself. A place of Challenge. Inspiration. Mission. Finding Jesus. Music. Connecting. Personal Growth.

Visit and You Will Find…

- *Keith Green.* Read more about Keith's life story. Find out more about the heart behind his ministry and music. View personal photos at the Keith Green Photo Gallery. Read all of Keith's written messages. Find out about upcoming Keith Green projects. Order his books and CDs online.

- *Melody Green:* Melody's Ministry Schedule is posted, and she might be coming your way! Contact her for interviews or speaking engagements online or by mail. Find out about Melody's upcoming projects. Read her new messages, "Women Beyond the Cave", "You Are a Dangerous Generation" (Youth), "Why Aren't More People Getting Saved?"

- *Americans Against Abortion:* Discover our long pro-life history. Online you can read our many world-renowned pro-life materials, including Melody's tract "Children, Things We Throw Away?" with over 20 million in print and translated around the world. You can also order the impactful "Baby Choice" video with Melody and some tiny lives that didn't make it (this video was personally endorsed by President Reagan).

- *Other Website Sections:* Women In Ministry, 4 Youth By Youth, Into The Streets, Into The Nations, Hotlines for Help, connect with other ministries, and more.

More Ministry Materials Available Only from Us:

- *LDM Classic Tracts and NEW Articles:* Megabytes of FREE ministry materials to download or e-mail to friends. Hundreds of life-changing articles on relevant topics by Keith Green, Melody Green, John Dawson, Floyd McClung, Jack Hayford, Leonard Ravenhill, and many others. Also order our articles printed as tracts to hand out to others.

- *Keith Green Memorial Concert Video:* This is incredibly powerful! Includes 25 minutes of one of Keith's last concerts, home movies, Melody's account of the plane crash and God's mercy since then. It's really a life-changer. 58 min.

- *Keith Green Songbooks:* Learn to play and sing all the songs written by Keith and Melody, as recorded by Keith.

- *Keith Green and Melody Green Video and Audio Teachings:* Keith's teachings are classics and a must-see for anyone wanting to get fired up for a closer walk with the Lord. Also, Melody will be adding her current video messages to all that is already available. There are also great teachings from many others.

Order our ministry materials online for the quickest service.
Or request a Ministry Materials Catalog from: Last Days Ministries, 825 College Blvd., Suite 102 #333, Oceanside, CA 92057
Request a catalog by phone at: 1-800-228-9536

Our Ongoing Mission and Calling

"Our ministry is not about 'one issue,' but it is about 'one thing'—being totally committed to Jesus, reaching the world with His love, and encouraging others to do the same. In light of this:

- "We will challenge believers to radical Christianity and spiritual growth while not neglecting those who don't know Jesus. We will challenge them to go beyond the walls of their church to reach the poor, the hurting, and the lost…in their neighborhoods, areas of natural influence, and in foreign lands.

- "We will try to express the things we believe are on the Lord's heart for the hour in which we live. We will do our very best to follow the Holy Spirit and address the issues we believe the Lord wants us to highlight, in a thoughtful and prayerful way.

- "We will do all we can to promote genuine revival—encouraging believers to serve and pray together so God's Kingdom can grow as we walk in humility and in unity.

- "We will encourage believers to fulfill their destiny regardless of their gender, age, culture, race, or nationality. All believers have a destiny to fulfill as they love and worship God. We want to be a source of inspiration to help them do it."

—Melody Green, 2001

About Melody Green:

Melody Green is the Co-Founder and President of Last Days Ministries. As an international speaker and author she has traveled to over 35 countries. Also a gifted songwriter, Melody has composed classic songs such as "There Is A Redeemer" and "Make My Life A Prayer To You"—with more than 30 other songs recorded. Currently she is excited over speaking about the extreme calling on this generation, the power of genuine worship, and challenging believers to reach beyond the walls of their churches to the hurting, the lost, and this emerging generation.

Melody also teaches songwriting and often shares her testimony of God's faithfulness since the death of her husband Keith and their two small children. Comfortable with a wide-ranging ministry, Melody connects well with all ages. She is featured on TV and radio, also at youth and career-age groups, and at conferences, rallies, and churches.

Photo courtesy of
Jerry Bryant